San Francisco Chronicle

Unforgettable!

The Giants' spectacular 2002 pennant-winning season

By the staff of The San Francisco Chronicle

TRIUMPH
BOOKS
CHICAGO

CONTENTS

San Francisco Giants slugger Barry Bonds, before hitting his milestone 600th home run this season. In pursuit of the all-time home run mark, Bonds is behind Hank Aaron, Babe Ruth and Willie Mays.

San Francisco Chronicle

John Oppedahl PUBLISHER, CHAIRMAN AND CEO
Phil Bronstein SENIOR VICE PRESIDENT AND EXECUTIVE EDITOR
Narda Zacchino ASSISTANT EXECUTIVE EDITOR
Robert Rosenthal MANAGING EDITOR
Kenn Altine ASSOCIATE MANAGING EDITOR

BOOK STAFF

Unforgettable! The Giants spectacular 2002 pennant-winning season

Editor: Andrew Pollack
Associate Editor: Leslie Guevarra
Copy Editor: Spud Hilton
Creative Director: Nanette Bisher
Designers: Matt Petty, Dorothy A. Yule

Director of Photography: Susan Gilbert
Photo Editor: Kathleen Hennessy
Photo production: Chris Hardy
Consultant: Brad Zucroff
Sports Editor: Glenn Schwarz

The cover: Dusty Baker and Kirk Rueter lead the Giants off the field after their playoff win in Atlanta. Photo by Carlos Avila Gonzalez / The Chronicle

Title page photo: J.T. Snow leaps for joy after the final out in the playoff series against the Braves. Photo by Deanne Fitzmaurice / The Chronicle

Back cover: Michael Macor / The Chronicle

This book is available in quantity at special discounts for your group or organization. For further information, contact:

Triumph Books
601 South LaSalle Street
Suite 500
Chicago, Illinois 60605
(312) 939-3330
Fax (312) 663-3557

Printed in the United States of America

ISBN 1-57243-562-3

MEMORABLE JOURNEY

Wearing pride instead of a ring

Giants' best season in 40 years not defined by its last games

By Bruce Jenkins
CHRONICLE STAFF WRITER

Feeling somewhat alone in the expanse of Anaheim red, Giants general manager Brian Sabean found a kindred spirit before Game 7 of the World Series.

"We're either going to be the happiest people in the world tonight," he told broadcaster Duane Kuiper, "or the proudest."

And so there was pride. In time. The first order of business was abject despair.

People hadn't seen the full range of Dusty Baker's emotions during his 10-year reign as the Giants' manager, just the prerequisite joy, anger and stoic observation. It was a different Baker as the team returned home that Monday morning, a man unable to contain his tears. For the few people who witnessed the scene, Baker's breakdown said everything about the incredible 2002 season.

It seems that Dusty was OK until he ran into Orlando Cepeda, that great Giant of the late 1950s and early '60s, before boarding the team bus headed for the Orange County airport. Dusty got a big hug from the "Baby Bull," then he lost it. The tears welled up, and they just kept coming. Baker was wiping his eyes along the freeway, on the plane flight and back home at Pacific Bell Park, where he found himself unable to address the 5,000 fans who had arrived for the team's official farewell.

For those few precious moments, private as they were, Baker connected with everyone in the Giants' realm — players, management and fans. Some wept openly, some threw pots and pans, some put up the brave front, some withdrew into quiet depression, but nobody was quite the same after the '02 World Se-

Giants manager Dusty Baker, holding his son, Darren, fights back tears after the post-World Series rally at Pacific Ball Park.

ries. People had never felt so wonderful about the team — or so crestfallen, all within a week's time. These Giants erased the bitter memories of postseasons past, reached the very pinnacle of hometown spirit, then descended into a dark, cavernous place, deeper and more disturbing than ever before.

Fittingly, there would be two reactions to such a development, operating on equal strength. As owner Peter Magowan said after the Angels' back-to-back wins to clinch the title, "This is a game that will break your heart. It just broke mine."

But Sabean's words ring true, as well. Game 7 is the center of the baseball universe. The Giants got there, fighting ridiculous odds along the way. Time will remind them that they were the National League champions, and that they gave San Francisco a brand of sustained excitement

reminiscent of the 49ers' finest hours.

The season began like so many in the Giants' recent history, a largely veteran group depending on experience, moderately good pitching and the unparalleled weaponry of Barry Bonds. Baker, coming off successful prostate-cancer surgery, was admittedly tired. He made certain to limit his exposure to the intense spring-training sunlight. Behind the scenes, people wondered if he'd be up for the long haul. But he felt good about the season, and his life, thinking to himself that "something big" was coming.

The Giants were picked to finish second behind defending world champion Arizona, and that's just what they did. But they turned their second-place finish into a wild-card playoff spot, and they did so with a flourish, winning 25 of their last 33 games and the last eight in a row. All the sweeter, they won a

head-to-head duel with the hated Dodgers to get there.

Only Bonds had a particularly exceptional season, and it nearly defied description. With 46 home runs and a .370 average, earning him the batting title, he put together the best power-average combination since Babe Ruth in 1931. He was now Ruth, once again, with touches of Ted Williams and Stan Musial thrown in. And there were times when it seemed he would be walked, intentionally or otherwise, every single trip to the plate.

A highly significant Baker move in June — moving Jeff Kent into the third slot, with Bonds shifting to fourth — kick-started Kent into his sixth consecutive 100-RBI season. New third baseman David Bell was a beacon of intelligence, hustle and clutch hitting. Kenny Lofton, the onetime Cleveland great acquired on the cheap in July, occasionally showed his age but proved to be a long-sought answer in the leadoff spot.

At the onset of the playoffs, people figured the Giants were delighted just to be there. That was hardly the case. With a cold, ruthless attack led by Bonds, suddenly unstoppable in October after a career's worth of postseason misery, they dispatched the mighty Atlanta Braves in the best-of-five Division Series. It was grim and harrowing, going right down to a first-and-third, nobody-out predicament for reliever Robb Nen in the ninth inning, but in a flash, he struck out Gary Sheffield and retired Chipper Jones on a series-ending double play.

At that moment, everything changed. "Once I got through Atlanta," said Bonds, long tormented by the Braves' dynasty, "nothing could bother me."

The National League Championship Series, against the St. Louis Cardinals, brought one of the greatest home weekends of the Giants' history. Bonds hit a massive three-run homer in Game 3 — a loss, as it turned out — and Benito Santiago came back the following night with a game-deciding two-run shot, giving the Giants a 3-1 series lead and himself the distinction of hitting the most significant home run of the club's 45 years in San Francisco.

Then came Game 5, the third session of pure delirium at Pac Bell Park, and the stunning sequence of two-out singles in the ninth: First Bell, then Shawon Dunston, and then Lofton, a picturesque liner to right field that scored Bell with a glorious headfirst slide.

The Giants Win the Pennant. It was the definitive phrase in franchise history, the immortal words of announcer Russ Hodges from "The Shot Heard 'Round the World" in 1951. Now it had returned, in living color. And by this time, the Giants had fully distanced themselves from the mediocre-looking outfit that struggled through the summer.

J.T. Snow engineered a sensational career revival, coming up with profound hits, great defensive plays and a world of inspiration when the team needed him most. Two-out hits were now commonplace, not fantasy. It seemed that every time Baker called on one of his old-timers, like Santiago or Dunston, they came through mightily.

David Bell scores the winning run in Game 5 against St. Louis, opposite page; above, Kenny Lofton exults after the game. Right, J.T. Snow flips the ball to first base for an out during the Cardinals series.

And the pitching rotation of Russ Ortiz, Jason Schmidt, Kirk Rueter and Livan Hernandez, while lacking a traditional ace, held stout and firm. People around the country were becoming aware of a disturbing subplot — the Baker-Magowan feud, leaving the manager's status in great peril — but this was the best team in the league, eminently ready for the World Series.

On a chilly Wednesday night, October 23, things reached a heady peak at Pac Bell. As the team willed its way to a 4-3 lead over the Angels, squaring the Series at 2-all, the downtown City Hall square was bathed in the soft light of Giants orange. Inside the opera house, the lead tenor opened the second act of a Mozart composition by singing the final score in German. At show's end, patrons spilled onto the sidewalks to the accompaniment of horn-honking and the shouts of victory. There was no way life could get better — except it did.

Game 5 of the 2002 World Series was the crowning moment of all San Francisco Giants lore, even more so than the Will Clark single against Mitch Williams in '89 or the stirring playoff series against the Dodgers in '62, giving the city its first World Series. This would be the last night of the home season, and the Giants crushed the Angels, 16-4. There was nothing left for the home fans to do, except hug each other and throw festive parties and toast what surely would be the team's first world championship.

To revisit the cruel, disastrous Game 6 would be to wallow in the melancholy. The players denied it, but Game 7 seemed an afterthought after that horrible Saturday night when the Giants blew a 5-0, seventh-inning lead with the champagne in their grasp. It all added up to a richly deserved championship for the Angels, a team of marvelous talent and resolve, and a shell-shocked group of Giants.

If anything, the mood had worsened by morning. People in the organization wore the look of irrevocable depression. Traveling fans, who had mixed a few smiles with their alcohol, seemed badly hung over. And Dusty Baker cried. That's when the revival process began, right then. It was a healing of the spirit and a resurrection of moments — wild, unforgettable episodes — that had set the stage. What just transpired, everyone could agree, was one hell of a baseball season. ◆

While still approaching 600 home runs, Giants slugger Barry Bonds waits on-deck during a game against the Colorado Rockies.

MICHAEL MACOR / THE CHRONICLE

CHAPTER 1

GIANTS LORE

Cross-country rivalry ends as battle of inches

Giants lose to Yankees in Series of 'what might have been'

OCT. 19. 2002

By Dwight Chapin
CHRONICLE SENIOR WRITER

The dream died in an instant. Willie McCovey swung, that big, thunderous swing, and the ball was a blur as it headed for right field, the hopes of Giants' fans along for what oh-so-briefly looked like a joy ride.

Then, in a bit of still-vivid World Series drama, the ball disappeared, into the glove of Yankees' second baseman Bobby Richardson.

"Everyone thinks I made a great catch," Richardson, who was shaded toward second on the play, would say later. "But the ball was hit right at me. It would have hit me right in the face if I didn't catch it."

Figuratively, it was the Giants' faithful that were smacked in the face.

One of the reasons that this was such a blow was that San Francisco hadn't had time to become blase about major league baseball. The Giants had been transplanted from New York in 1958, and this was 1962, and their first World Series since the move West.

After the Giants narrowly beat the Dodgers in a three-game playoff to win the National League pennant and reach the Fall Classic, thousands of enthusiastic fans swarmed the San Francisco airport. The crowd was so large that the players couldn't reach the terminal, and a number of them had to hitchhike to get home.

So the '62 Series, at least for San Franciscans, was a huge thing.

These were old foes, the Yankees and Giants, teams that had met in the Series six times in New York, going back to 1921. But there was a different feel to it this time, because the clubs were now cross-country rather than cross-town rivals.

The Yankees got a quick jump in Game 1, when Whitey Ford went all the way for a 6-2 victory at Candlestick. But

'62 STARTERS

No.	Player	HR	RBI	AVG
C	Tom Haller	18	55	.26
1B	Orlando Cepeda	35	114	.30
2B	Chuck Hiller	3	48	.27
3B	Jim Davenport	14	58	.29
SS	Jose Pagan	7	57	.25
CF	Willie Mays	49	141	.30
RF	Felipe Alou	25	98	.31
LF	Harvey Kuenn	10	68	.30

PITCHERS

Billy O'Dell, LP (19-14)

Jack Sanford, RP (24-7)

Juan Marichal, RP (18-11)

Billy Pierce, LP (16-6)

Mike McCormick, LP (5-5)

Jack Sanford, who had won 24 games in the regular season, including 16 in a row at one point, came back with a three-hitter as the Giants took Game 2 2-0.

New York won two of the next three games, at Yankee Stadium, behind complete games from Bill Stafford and Ralph Terry. The Giants took Game 4, 7-3 when light-hitting second Chuck Hiller who had just three home runs in the regular season, connected for a seventh-inning grand slam.

Action came to an abrupt halt when the teams returned to San Francisco, a rain delayed Game 6 for three days. But left-hander Billy Pierce, one of the least recognized pitching stars of the 1950 and 1960s, pitched a three-hitter to beat Hall-of-Famer-to-be Ford, 5-2.

And that led to the climactic seventh game, Terry against Sanford for the third time in the Series.

Both pitchers were almost invulnera

e. The Yankees squeaked out a run on double-play grounder in the fifth. The Giants got nothing through eight innings, generating only two hits.

Then, in the ninth, Matty Alou led off with a bunt hit, and, after the next two Giants were retired, Willie Mays doubled into the right-field corner. But Alou was held at third, a crucial development.

"The field was wet and it slowed the ball down," Mays said. "Roger Maris [he Yanks' right fielder] was able to get . On a dry field, the run scores."

Third base coach Whitey Lockman, who held up Alou, said, "Only the good ord knows, but if I'd sent him, I think he would have been out by 10 feet."

So it came down to McCovey against Terry, the mighty swing, the laser line drive, the Richardson catch that probably was as much self defense as skill.

"One foot either way and it's a hit," McCovey said. "But there was nothing I could do about it."

The Giants wouldn't return to the World Series until 1989, when an earthquake rather than a rain delay got in the way. They almost didn't show up in that one, being swept in four games by the A's.

So it's 1962 that sticks most tantalizingly in the memory, an everlasting What Might Have Been? ◆

Giants, earth both shaken in '89 Series

A's were dominant team, quake is dominant memory

OCT. 19, 2002

By Ron Kroichick
CHRONICLE STAFF WRITER

Thirteen years later, history does the Giants no favors. The numbers still reflect an utterly lopsided October duel, with San Francisco on the wrong end of the equation. Not even an epic earthquake changes that.

The earthquake, of course, is what most people remember about the 1989 World Series, the last time the Giants reached this grand sporting stage.

Baseball slides neatly into the background, an unfortunate slice of reality for the A's.

Fact is, the gentlemen from Oakland rolled to a four-game sweep with clinical efficiency. The A's outscored the Giants 32-14; never trailed in the series; and even varied their method, showing off a tidy package of pitching, defense, power and speed.

And the most vivid images still involve the crumpled freeway in Oakland, fires in the Marina, the sagging Bay Bridge — tragedy all around, forever linked with the World Series.

"The tragedy of that Series is all the people who lost their lives (67 in all) and the damage to the infrastructure of the cities," former Giants general manager Al Rosen said in 1999, for a Chronicle story about the 10-year anniversary of the '89 Series.

"I really remember more about that than I do about the playing of the games."

The quake struck at 5:04 p.m. on Tuesday, Oct. 17, exactly 31 minutes before the scheduled start of Game 3 at Candlestick Park. As a national television audience watched the pregame

'89 STARTERS

No.	Player	HR	RBI	AV
C	Terry Kennedy	5	34	.23
1B	Will Clark	23	111	.33
2B	Robby Thompson	13	50	.24
3B	Ernest Riles*	7	40	.27
3B	Matt Williams	18	50	.20
SS	Jose Uribe	1	30	.22
OF	Brett Butler	4	36	.28
OF	Kevin Mitchell	47	125	.29
OF	C. Maldonado	9	41	.21

*DH in World Series

PITCHERS

Rick Reuschel, RP(17-8)
Don Robinson, RP (12-11)
Scott Garrelts, RP (14-5)
Kelly Downs, RP (4-8)

show, Mother Nature rudely interrupte ABC broadcaster Al Michaels.

That quickly, the biggest sportin event in Bay Area history becam strangely irrelevant.

Players milled about on the field, a baseball officials scrambled to gather i formation. Once the damage in the Ba Area was clear, Commissioner Fay Vi cent postponed the game.

"The first thing I think of is all th people standing on the field," former A pitcher Dave Stewart said. "I rememb watching the light standards sway, li tening to all the chaos going on aroun me. I don't really remember much pa the first two games and the earthquake.

Stewart probably remembers Game because he controlled it. He tossed complete-game, five-hit shutout at th Coliseum, giving the A's an early edg Mike Moore followed suit, stifling th Giants in Game 2.

Then came the earthquake, which ultimately pushed Game 3 back 10 days.

A's manager Tony La Russa, still stinging from his team's World Series pratfall a year earlier against the Dodgers, kept his club sharp by playing several intrasquad games during the delay.

Dennis Eckersley drilled Jose Canseco between the shoulder blades in one of those intrasquad games. Nobody called the pitch intentional, even in retrospect, but Eckersley and Canseco were never fast friends — and Eckersley had legendary control.

As nervous coaches stepped between them, Eckersley and Canseco traded loud, angry words. This was not part of

La Russa's plan, obviously, but his team clearly would not slip into complacency this time.

The Giants discovered that on Oct. 27, when the Series finally resumed at Candlestick. Scott Garrelts, who had absorbed the loss against Stewart in Game 1, did the same in Game 3. The A's jumped on Garrelts for four runs, then kept up the assault against a parade of relievers.

This time, it was all about power: Oakland launched five homers in its 13-7 victory, matching a Series record set by the New York Yankees in 1928.

Rickey Henderson christened Game 4 with another homer, connecting against Giants starter Don Robinson. Off went

the A's, completing their sweep with an emphatic 9-6 win, culminating in Eckersley taking a throw from second baseman Tony Phillips to secure the title.

All the while, San Francisco's powerful tandem of Will Clark and Kevin Mitchell stayed remarkably quiet. Clark and Mitchell combined for 336 RBIs during the regular season, but they had exactly two in the World Series — both coming on a home run by Mitchell in Game 4, after the A's had moved comfortably ahead.

"In retrospect, the '89 A's were one of the best teams I've ever seen," former Giants pitcher Mike Krukow said. "They were unbelievable. They did not have a weakness." ◆

Series on hold: Officials, players and police stand on the field at Candlestick after the quake, above right, including Oakland's Carney Lansford, above left. Opposite page, the destruction in the Marina District. Top, shell-shocked Giants sit in the dugout during Game 2.

Many memories waiting to happen

Pacific Bell Ballpark opens with the promise of new sagas for years to come

APRIL 12, 2000

The memories of a place are never written in their openings.

It takes time, and events, to carve out a legacy. We will recall that we were there at Pac Bell Park on the Giants' long-awaited opening day, and perhaps that managing general partner Peter Magowan threw out the first pitch.

The "I was there" T-shirts will fade slowly after years of washing. But the stories we will tell our children, and grandchildren, are yet to happen. This will change once the red, white and blue bunting comes down, and the opening ceremonies consist of no more than batting practice and the exchange of lineup cards.

We will learn the best routes to the park, become comfortable with the stroll through the city streets. Popcorn will be spilled, Dodgers will be booed, and when someone hits one hard to the deepest part of the park, as Giants catcher Doug Mirabelli did in the second inning yesterday, we will nudge the person next to us and say, wisely, "Watch. This could be a triple."

It was.

There is always something overdone and artificial about grand openings, and

C.W. NEVIUS

yesterday was no exception. There were roaring jet flyovers, the hearty belting of "San Francisco" by Val Diamond from "Beach Blanket Babylon," and dignified tooting from the tuxedoed members of the San Francisco Symphony horn section. There were parachutists, American flags, followed by even larger flags.

All very nice. But some time after comedians Robin Williams and Jonathan Winters stepped out of their limo, and movie star Danny Glover concluded a dramatic reading, something began to happen.

A bag of peanuts was tossed by a vendor in Section 117. A damp puddle of spilled beer began to appear on the floor of the Promenade Concourse down the left field line. A father turned to a son, or a daughter, and asked, "Can you see OK?"

And about that time, Giants outfielder Barry Bonds lined a hooking shot due south that kicked off the pure, perfect grass in right field and clanged off chain fence like the bell of a new morning.

That's when it really started.

"All I can say," said Giants' manager Dusty Baker after the 6-5 win by the Dodgers, "is you ain't seen nothin' yet."

This is a good thing. Let the beer-spilling begin. Already we are starting to get the hang of this.

Do you remember the time, again the Dodgers, when Barry Bonds took foul ball right off his right instep, an got up off the ground to hit one awa and gone over the center-field fence Some 40,930 fans do. It happened ye terday in the third inning, about the tim we all noticed that a ballgame was tal ing place.

Already, some truths are self-eviden The wind, for example, is still a facto About 1:30 yesterday afternoon, Mik Mosely, a project superintendent for th construction pointed out to the weathe vane in center field.

"See that?" he said as the arro swung back and forth. "Sometimes gets so confused that it starts to spi around. There isn't much wind in th morning, but it picks up in the afte noon, and then dies after dark."

Still, someone like Jim McCormic claims that the wind at Pac Bell is " piece of cake compared to Candlestick. Everybody has an opinion about th wind, of course, except that McCormic is one of the few who started his con

Where Giants walk the earth: Pacific Bell Park, from left, during its evolution from muddy field to shapeless superstructure to identifiable complex to jewel of San Francisco's waterfront and home of the Giants. The park was privately funded.

Pitcher Robb Nen
signs autographs
for the crowds of
construction
workers, right,
as the
field begins to
take shape.
Above, Opening
Day ceremonies
at Pacific Bell
Park on
April 11, 2000.

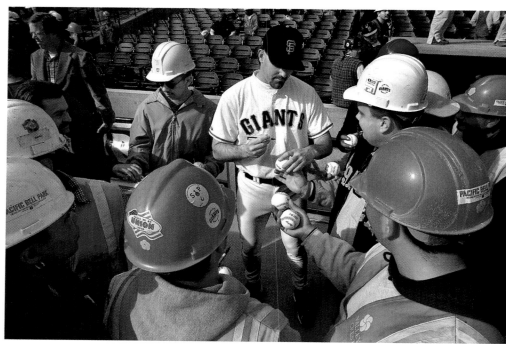

There will be better stories here. Some will involve the wind, or the water, or even defeat. The Giants will be at Pac Bell Park tonight, tomorrow night and the night after that. They will win, and lose, and create a new saga every year. Our job is just to wait, and watch.

mute to the park at a height of 4,000 feet.

"I am," he said, "the first sky diver to jump into both Pac Bell and Candlestick Park."

Which would also have been true of his fellow parachutist, Jim Wallace, except that he got caught in the currents and realized he wasn't going to clear the scoreboard. So he set his parasail, with the American flag he was hauling, into the vacant lot behind left field. No big deal, Wallace said. But then skydivers tend to take these moments in stride.

"We were wondering if we hit the water," McCormick said, "would it count on the 'splash hits' scoreboard in right field."

The wind we expected. The water comes as a bit of a surprise. The nine-inning session of bumper boats out in McCovey Cove is the second best show in China Basin.

Yesterday there were jet skis, kayaks, sailboats, cabin cruisers, and a guy on a surfboard wearing a banana costume. The rule is no anchoring, so the boats are constantly shifting, bumping each other, fighting the current.

At any given moment there are several thousand people who are leaning on the Promenade railing, with their backs to the game, just watching the maneuvering. They knew, of course, that if anything important happened, they could catch the replay on the video screen in center field.

In the long run, they didn't miss much. Nobody is going to dine out on the strength of his story about how he was at the game when Kevin Elster hit three home runs.

"Guy hits three home runs to initial the ballpark," said Baker, shaking his head, "I don't think I've ever seen that."

There will be better stories here. Some will involve the wind, or the water, or even defeat. The Giants will be at Pac Bell Park tonight, tomorrow night and the night after that. They will win, and lose, and create a new saga every year. Our job is just to wait, and watch.

The best news is, we've got great seats and a great location. When J.T. Snow lobbed one up into the short porch in right field in the bottom of the ninth to cut the Dodger lead to one run, the roars could be heard in the Financial District.

Meanwhile, somewhere at Candlestick Park, a hot dog wrapper blew across an empty infield. ◆

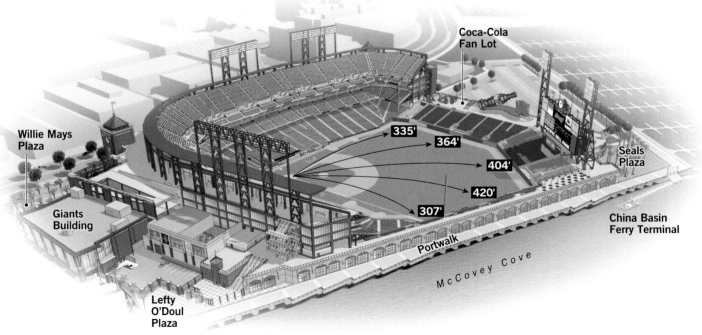

Surgery doesn't cut into Baker's season

Giants skipper confident after having cancerous prostate removed

DEC. 18, 2001

By Ron Kroichick
CHRONICLE STAFF WRITER

Giants manager Dusty Baker had successful surgery yesterday to remove his cancerous prostate. Baker, 52, underwent the three-hour procedure at Stanford Hospital after a biopsy in early November uncovered the cancer.

The Giants released a statement saying that team physicians Brad Maring and Reggie Rector discovered the cancer in its early stage. A biopsy yesterday on the surrounding lymph nodes was negative.

The team described Baker's prognosis as "extremely positive." He is expected to regain full strength by the start of spring training in mid-February.

Giants trainer Stan Conte joined Baker at the hospital, as did Baker's wife, Melissa, his father, Johnnie, and his brother, Vic.

"Dusty was very upbeat," Conte said. "He was confident, that's probably the best word. He felt confident with the doctor and with the decision to have surgery."

The surgery, performed by Dr. Joseph Presti, occurred barely two months after Baker took his routine postseason physical the second week of October. Conte said Baker and all Giants coaches are given PSA tests as part of the physical, to test for the presence of a protein called prostate specific antigen.

Baker's level of PSA was above normal, so team doctors then performed the biopsy and found the cancerous cells.

That prompted Baker to launch a monthlong research project. His quest started close to home, because his father was diagnosed with prostate cancer several years ago. Johnnie Baker Sr. underwent treatment for the cancer, but he did not have surgery.

Dusty Baker also spoke at length with New York Yankees manager Joe Torre, a prostate-cancer survivor. Torre was diagnosed early in spring training in 1999. He had surgery to remove the prostate on March 18, 1999, prompting him to miss the first 36 games of the season.

Torre gave Baker a lot of information and help as he contemplated surgery, Conte said.

"That gave him a lot of confidence to think the surgery was really going to be OK," Conte said.

Baker and Torre are among the most active major-league managers in raising funds for prostate-cancer research. Baker was one of the first managers to become involved in the CapCure Home-Run Challenge, a program that raises money through pledges per home run during 60 selected major-league games the week of Father's Day.

Baker kept his diagnosis mostly private, informing only a few Giants officials.

"This is scary. It's scary for you, me or anybody, and the younger you are, the more dangerous it is," said Giants

Scheduling his prostate surgery for late last year allowed Dusty Baker time to recover before the Giants' spring training in Scottsdale, Arizona. Baker spends time with his son, Darren, 3, above, and with the fans at Scottsdale Stadium, left.

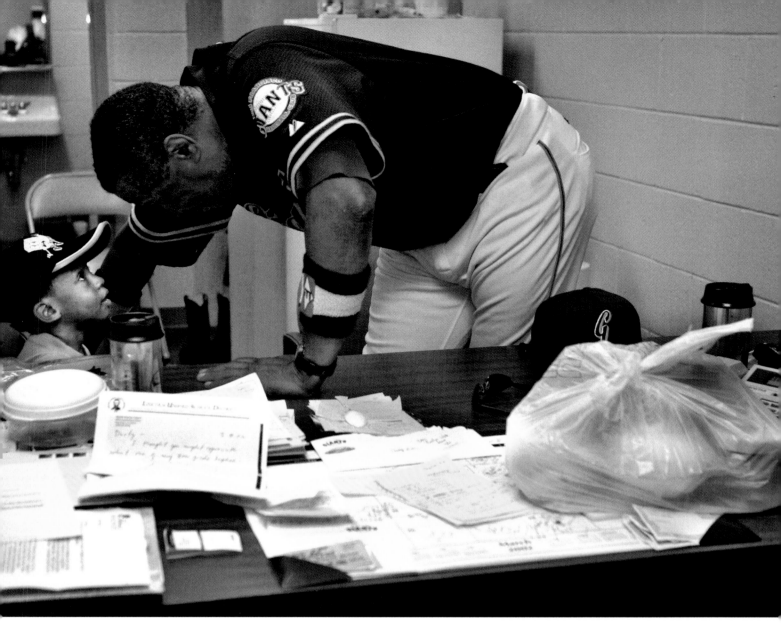

vner Peter Magowan, who spoke to elissa Baker after the operation. Dusty has a history of this in his fam- y, but the important thing is being in e right hands for his medical care. om what Melissa told me, the doctors e very encouraged."

Said team executive vice president rry Baer: "Dusty is a dear person to many people in our organization. e's such a part of our family. We're all inking the best for him."

Outfielder Shawon Dunston, who es in Fremont, learned of Baker's ill- ss yesterday from a reporter.

"Bake keeps stuff quiet and that's w it should be," Dunston said. Bake's a good man. He takes care of mself. All he does is eat fruit on the nch, and he's always eating three eals a day: breakfast, lunch and din- r."

Dunston has no doubts Baker will come through this ordeal.

"He's been fighting all his life. He's sat down and talked to me about things and said this (baseball) ain't pressure," Dunston said. "It's time for him to be with his family and hear from nobody else. In a week or so, I'll probably call him and laugh and joke and see how he's doing."

Conte said Baker will spend two to three days in the hospital, then will con- valesce at home for about two weeks. Conte said patients usually return to full strength from this surgery in four to six weeks; that's one reason Baker chose to have the surgery now, to give him more than eight weeks before spring work- outs begin in Arizona on Feb. 15.

Baker has managed the Giants for nine years. He is a three-time National League manager of the year, and his 745 victories are the most in San Francisco history. ◆

HE'S A WINNER

Dusty Baker's 840-715 record as the Giants manager is second in wins to John McGraw, who has a 2,604-1,801 record. Baker's year-by-year regular season record and finish in division:

Year	W	L	Finish
1993	103	59	2nd
1994	55	60	2nd
1995	67	77	4th
1996	68	94	4th
1997	90	72	1st
1998	89	74	2nd
1999	86	76	2nd
2000	97	65	1st
2001	90	72	2nd
2002	95	66	2nd*

*Wild-card winner

Making sure Bonds' midlife isn't a crisis

Slugger will have to decide when he — and his welcome — are worn out

JAN. 15, 2002

Barry Bonds, now officially signed up to play baseball until age 41, said he couldn't take his eyes off the TV Saturday night, when 39-year-old Jerry Rice sprinted circles around the New York Jets. Bonds said he shouted at the screen.

"Go on, old man, get 'em," Bonds said last night, reliving his moment of kinship with Rice.

Bonds always has been a fan of other superstars. Several years ago, when Michael Jordan visited the Warriors, Bonds stood outside the locker room waiting patiently to meet Jordan, eager as any admirer.

Rice and Jordan might be Bonds' role models right now. Both are on the cusp of 40 and playing, if not at their peaks, better than most youngsters in their games.

The problem is, Bonds can't copy the current editions of Rice and Jordan. His $90 million contract rules out that. Rice and Jordan left the teams of their glory days. To extend their careers, they put on new uniforms and, more important, took salaries unworthy of superstars.

Their paychecks guaranteed that they couldn't turn into decrepit liabilities. Bonds' deal means that he will have to know when to pull the plug on his career, and he will have to be less tolerant than most aging legends, less willing to accept decline.

"You don't have to worry," he said at the news conference to announce his deal. "If I can't play, I'll leave gracefully."

He made the same promise when Mark McGwire retired last fall, with McGwire admitting that his injuries had made him an obstacle to the Cardinals' success. Bonds vowed that if he broke down like McGwire did in 2001 — three years after breaking Roger Maris' single-season home-run record — he wouldn't force the Giants to keep swallowing his salary.

If Bonds doesn't hold himself to that, his legacy could be tainted forever. In general, that's not true of older players who hang on. It's just what sportswriters say, forgetting that history is kinder to athletes than they are.

When he aged and stumbled, Willie Mays could sit on the bench, if necessary. His last year, his time with the Mets, didn't hurt his legacy, not in any real way.

Does anyone hear Mays' name and think of him as a faded star? No, everyone sees him making an over-the-shoulder catch, proving himself as the greatest player of his day.

GWEN KNAPP

Giants owner Peter Magowan insisted several times last night that Bonds' fat contract would not keep the franchise from spending money to flesh out other positions. Magowan said he thought the 2002 team would be the best San Francisco had seen in 10 years. Of course, no one expected him to say that he had sold out the future of the club to keep a single player who happens to be a great gate attraction.

If Bonds ends up seriously chasing Hank Aaron's 755 home runs, Magowan will have made a sound business investment. Bonds, though, has to preserve his status as a player, not as a marketing tool. He can't hang around just to break records. He has to be leading the Giants forward.

Imagine that Bonds goes into the fifth season of the deal, with his talent fully in decline but his home-run total at 735. Is it worth keeping him around to get 20 more? The only way to answer yes is if the Giants won a World Series the year before, if he avoided becoming Ernie Banks before he set his sights on Aaron.

The Giants and Bonds both trumpeted their decision to let the team void the fifth year of the deal, the year he turns 42, if Bonds has lost the ability to be an everyday player. But what if he starts to falter sooner? What if at age 40, he actually plays like a 40-year-old?

He undoubtedly will stay in shape. He always has. He also is a wizard at playing through the aches that afflict baseball players of all ages.

At his news conference, Bonds was wearing a huge diamond ring engraved with the number 73, a gift from a friend, a reminder of his bumper crop of homers at age 37. It also was a reminder of why he can demand to play until age 41, and expect to keep going longer.

"Is 40, 50 home runs enough for you?" he asked reporters last night, reminding them not to write him off for being excellent rather than record-shattering.

Ultimately, though, Bonds has to answer that question for himself. Whatever he does, is it enough to justify his salary? It will be his call, his chore to watch for age creeping up on him. ◆

Barry Bonds jokes with baseball great Willie Mays, right, during a ceremony to celebrate Barry Bonds' 73 home runs last season. Above, the ring Bonds wears – with the "73" in diamonds – to mark the feat.

Spring trading

GM Sabean shuffles, deals a promising team

FEB. 23, 2002

Giants General Manager Brian Sabean has conducted a seminar this off-season in putting together a team.

At the end of last season, the Giants were a flawed, aging team with little hope for the future. It would have been catastrophic on the field and at the box office if the Giants had been unable to re-sign Barry Bonds, the leading offensive force in the game. Yet, it seemed that re-signing Bonds would be so costly it would prevent the Giants from addressing their other problems, specifically below-average play in center field, right field and third base.

But Sabean managed to solve all those problems, and the Giants will go to spring training this month with a team that owner Peter Magowan calls the best since he and his partners bought the franchise in late 1992.

GLENN DICKEY

Here's how Sabean did it:

■ The owners approved a jump in the payroll, to about $80 million, while Sabean and chief operating officer Larry Baer put together a creative package to sign Bonds, deferring significant amounts so the actual payout in any year will not exceed $15 million.

■ He traded problematic pitcher Shawn Estes to the New York Mets for center fielder Tsuyoshi Shinjo and infielder Desi Relaford. Estes would have gotten a huge raise this year because he was arbitration-eligible, and the Giants had tired of waiting for Estes to fulfill his potential.

"This was an on-going conversation," Sabean said. "The Mets had always been interested in Estes, and we felt this was the best deal we could make."

Shinjo is an outstanding defensive outfielder and a good baserunner, but his offense is questionable. "I'm not going to sit here and tell you he's an All-Star," said Sabean, "but he is a definite upgrade for us."

■ He took advantage of a depressed free-agent market to sign Reggie Sanders for a relatively cheap $1.5 million, giving the Giants a right fielder and a potent power hitter to hit behind Bonds and Jeff Kent.

"Sanders really just fell into our laps," Sabean said. "He wanted to stay in the National League and he had his eye on us, as he had last year before he signed with the Diamondbacks. I had to run this one by ownership, too, because we were already over budget, but they gave me the OK."

■ He traded Relaford to the Seattle Mariners for David Bell, who will give the Giants solid defense at third and decent hitting. "In essence, then, we traded Estes for Shinjo and Bell, which we're very happy about," Sabean said. "We had to get permission from Major League Baseball to work out a new deal with him before we could make the trade."

Sabean also picked up another good arm for the bullpen in Jay Witasick. Manager Dusty Baker and Sabean do not always agree, but they both believe a strong bullpen is a must in this era of starting pitchers who think it's a great accomplishment to pitch into the sixth inning.

A little sly trading – and a bigger budget – patched some weak spots. Among the new players are Reggie Sanders (left) and David Bell, above, as well as Jay Witasick.

The Giants still have questions — primarily whether J.T. Snow can bounce back from yet another injury and whether they can afford to rest Benito Santiago enough to keep his play from dropping off as it did in the second half of last season — but, overall, this looks like a very good team.

Sabean has been doing this every year since 1997, when he completely transformed the team by trading Matt Williams for Kent and others and trading for Snow.

The future is always now for the Giants. "We never look beyond this season," Sabean said. They are trying to turn a traditionally fickle fan base into a faithful one, which means they must be at least contenders every year, which means a largely veteran team and constant turnover from one year to the next.

Neither Sabean nor Baker have much patience with young players. Both speak glowingly of the potential of third baseman Pedro Feliz, but Sabean didn't hesitate to trade for Bell, which will delay Feliz's chance to be a regular for at least a year.

"Feliz is a victim of the rules," Sabean said. "He could really use another year in the minors, but he's out of options, so if I put him on waivers, somebody would claim him. We just have to hope that he can serve his apprenticeship and break through, like Rich Aurilia did."

The farm system has been producing pitchers but little else. Sabean's philosophy is that it's usually too expensive to trade for pitchers or sign them as free agents, but it's always possible to fill other positions by trading prospects.

His philosophy works. This year, it may get the Giants to their first World Series since 1989. ◆

Not your average 'Jo'

Style of Giants' latest import translates well at Pacific Bell Park

FEB. 13, 2002

By Henry Schulman
CHRONICLE STAFF WRITER

Tsuyoshi Shinjo strode into his introductory news conference at Pacific Bell Park yesterday wearing a natty gray sports coat, a black turtleneck shirt and a pair of sunglasses that cost as much as a backup infielder. His perfectly coiffed hair was dyed auburn, and his humor was as sharp as his appearance.

Shinjo's task at spring training, which begins Friday, is to prove he is the center fielder and leadoff hitter the Giants need. The club can only hope his substance on the field matches his style in street clothes.

Shinjo is confident, perfectly comfortable with his transoceanic celebrity and quite witty, even through a translator.

When asked about playing for the same team that made Masanori Murakami the first Japanese-born major-leaguer, Shinjo said, "I took a tour of Pacific Bell Park and I saw a picture of him eating his first hot dog in the States. I want the Giants someday to put up some pictures of me eating a sandwich or something."

When asked what he preferred to be called, Shinjo said, "My first name is Tsuyoshi. The 'Tsu' sound is tough for the American people to pronounce. They pronounce it 'Tu.' So I think I like 'Shinjo,' or 'Jo.' It's easier for the American people."

On his offense with the Mets last year: "My batting average was like the city of San Francisco, going up the hill, down the hill."

He declared Howard Stern his favorite American TV personality and, when asked what he liked most about the United States, he replied, "Krispy Kremes."

General manager Brian Sabean rolled his eyes and said, "Keep him away from one of our pitchers." Sabean sees a lot more in Shinjo than a potential source of saturated fats for Livan Hernandez. Sabean sees Shinjo's acquisition as a long-overdue foray for the Giants into the increasingly valuable market for Japanese players. More immediately, Sabean views the 30-year-old as a significant defensive upgrade at a crucial position.

"This guy is going to take your breath away chasing down balls in center field," Sabean said. ◆

Giants GM Brian Sabean said of Tsuyoshi Shinjo, above at spring training, "This guy is going to take your breath away chasing down balls in center field."

The challenge

Owner Magowan makes bold prediction — weeks before spring training

FEB. 3, 2002

John Shea
CHRONICLE STAFF WRITER

Spring training doesn't start for two weeks, but it's never too early for owner Peter Magowan to declare his Giants the favorites in the National League West.

"I think we should be," he said in an interview yesterday. "I don't see any holes on the team."

Magowan was at Fort Mason for the team's annual "fanfest," an opportunity for fans to wait in long lines for tickets — 24 games already are sold out — and autographs, and he had no reservations about insisting the 2002 team is the best since he became boss a decade ago.

Even the presence of the Diamondbacks, who won the World Series in only their fourth season of existence, didn't deter Magowan from suggesting the Giants ought to be division champs.

THE MAGOWAN YEARS

The Giants have the sixth-best record in the major leagues since 1993 when Peter Magowan and his ownership group took over the team.

Team	W	L	Pct.
Atlanta	952	600	.630
N.Y. Yankees	922	627	.595
Cleveland	868	683	.559
Seattle	840	711	.541
Houston	840	714	.540
San Francisco	**840**	**715**	**.540**
Boston	829	731	.531
Los Angeles	819	735	.527

"Since we lost to the Diamondbacks by two games, we improved right field, center field, third base, starting pitching, relief pitching, defense and speed," he said.

"The Diamondbacks lost their right fielder, who hit 33 home runs — and they lost him to us."

That's Reggie Sanders, who signed as a free agent and will join two other lineup upgrades, center fielder Tsuyoshi Shinjo and third baseman David Bell. Jay Witasick was acquired for bullpen depth. As for the starting rotation, Jason Schmidt (acquired in a July trade) will be available an entire season.

"I think the Diamondbacks should be considered the favorites — by themselves," Magowan said.

'If they pick themselves or if sportswriters pick them, it's the easy pick. But what I look at is, what have they done to make themselves a better team vs. what have we done to make ourselves a better team."

The fact is, the Diamondbacks still have two entities the Giants don't, Curt Schilling and Randy Johnson, and no improvement is needed there. Plus they added Rick Helling as the No. 3 starter, leaving two spots for Brian Anderson and Miguel Batista unless Todd Stottlemyre is healthy.

Manager Dusty Baker, who attended yesterday's event — looking fit and trim in one of his first public appearances since his December operation to remove a cancerous prostrate gland — typically refused to rank his team among division foes.

"Everybody's gotten good," he said. "The Diamondbacks got better, as far as I'm concerned."

The Giants have won only one playoff game in the Magowan-Brian Sabean-Baker regime, and it's no secret one year

remains on Baker's and Sabean's contracts. So this may be the last chance for a group that includes second baseman Jeff Kent, who can be a free agent next winter.

It's doubtful Kent will sign an extension before opening day, Magowan said, and the team doesn't plan to negotiate during the season.

As for Baker, he just seems happy to return for a 10th season. "With what I've been through," he said, "you don't look too far ahead at anything. Just take it and appreciate what you have. I'm pretty lucky, really." ◆

Giants owner Peter Magowan (left) predicted his team would be the favorites of the National League.

Fast start

Opening Day drubbing of Los Angeles first of six straight for Giants

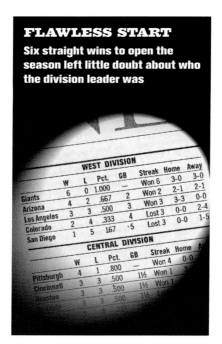

WEST DIVISION							
	W	L	Pct.	GB	Streak	Home	Away
Giants	6	0	1.000	—	Won 6	3-0	3-0
Arizona	4	2	.667	2	Won 2	2-1	2-1
Los Angeles	3	3	.500	3	Won 3	3-3	0-0
Colorado	2	4	.333	4	Lost 3	0-0	2-4
San Diego	1	5	.167	5	Lost 3	0-0	1-5

CENTRAL DIVISION							
	W	L	Pct.	GB	Streak	Home	A
Pittsburgh	4	1	.800	—	Won 4	0-0	
Cincinnati	3	3	.500	1½	Won 1		
Houston	3	3	.500	1½			

APRIL 3, 2002

By Henry Schulman
CHRONICLE STAFF WRITER

LOS ANGELES — Try for a moment to forget the two home runs that Barry Bonds hit in yesterday's season opener against the Los Angeles Dodgers. Squelch the temptation to start calculating the astronomical offensive possibilities for the left fielder after his five-RBI start.

Consider instead that the Giants' leadoff and cleanup hitters went a combined 0-for-8 with four strikeouts, yet the team still scored nine runs on 12 hits and sent Kevin Brown to the showers after four innings.

Contemplate the way embattled starter Livan Hernandez four-hit the Dodgers over eight innings.

Now you can understand why the Giants were so pumped about their 9-2 triumph at Dodger Stadium, a drubbing so comprehensive that it was difficult to pinpoint Bonds as the catalyst despite his best Opening Day ever.

"There's no question it takes a whole team to win games. It's going to have to be different people every day," second baseman David Bell said. "Over a long season, two or three guys can't do it all, so this was a great way to start out."

Bell wasted no time ingratiating himself to his new teammates. He singled to start a five-run rally in the second inning that let 53,356 fans know this was not going to be a typical Brown-beating of the Giants. An inning later, Bell homered.

Rich Aurilia and Hernandez also had two hits apiece off Brown. Hernandez's first single produced the Giants' first run, bringing Bell home to tie the score 1-1 in the second before Aurilia's two-out single gave the Giants a 2-1 lead.

Bonds then lashed the third pitch he saw this season the other way, into the left-field pavilion, for his first three RBIs.

In the fourth, he lined a single to right off Brown for his fourth RBI, then got No. 5 off Omar Daal in the seventh when he hit a stratospheric blast over the right-field foul pole and into the second deck for his second home run and an 8-2 Giants lead.

"If he doesn't walk 200 times this year, the league is crazy," Dodgers first baseman Eric Karros said.

It was like nothing had changed, as if the winter and spring training were merely a long off day for the man who blasted 73 home runs last year.

"That's what superstars do. He picked up where he left off last year," manager Dusty Baker said. When asked

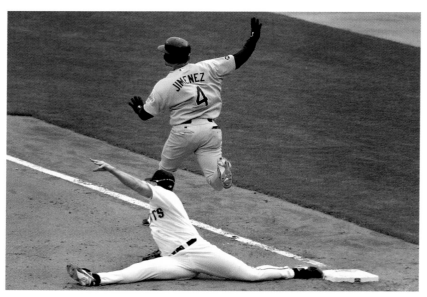

JEFF CHIU / THE CHRONICLE

terday morning, the media peppered Baker with questions about the decision. Fed up, Baker asked, "What's the next thing people are going to say, that he's too skinny? Everybody's going to say that if he doesn't pitch well."

He did pitch well.

After a shaky first three innings — he walked three in the second yet got out of it — Hernandez started to look like the pitcher who won 17 games two years ago. He threw a couple of fastballs that registered 94 mph on a generous radar gun.

Paul Lo Duca's double-play grounder in the third inning produced L.A.'s final run but also started a string of 14 hitters whom Hernandez retired. He struck out three, including Adrian Beltre on a curveball that had the Dodgers' third baseman bailing out of the box before it bent over the inside corner.

Hernandez said he was pumped up by the fans screaming at him as he warmed up in the visiting bullpen.

"That was a tough warm-up," pitching coach Dave Righetti said. "He was getting crushed. He held his composure great. When I saw that I said, 'He'll do good today.' He survived that first-inning-jitter thing, and that was it."

Time will tell if yesterday was a mirage. After all, Hernandez won last year's opener before sinking into despair, but the pitching coach is convinced.

"I didn't realize the uproar, that people were so against him starting (the opener)," Righetti said. "We weren't, obviously.

"We know what kind of kid this guy is. I thought he was on the right track in spring training. I thought he was pitching well and I thought he was capable of beating anyone," Righetti said. "He got us off to a great start." ◆

if he was surprised, Baker said, "He's hit 500-something home runs. It's kind of past surprising. You kind of accept it. It's definitely awesome, and you feel blessed to see it on your team."

Bonds deflected the credit for yesterday's victory to the Giants' starting pitcher.

"Livan won that game for us," Bonds said. "They got out on us early, but Livan kept them in check. Livan won that game. He doesn't do well in April and it was exciting to see him pitch well, especially against the Dodgers."

Baker named Hernandez the Opening Day starter despite the righthander's 10.50 ERA in spring training. The Bay Area's reaction was not kind. Even yes-

CHAPTER 3

Fights a factor in every family

JUNE 26, 2002

by Henry Schulman
CHRONICLE STAFF WRITER

Scuffle between Bonds, Kent — not their first — 'happens on good teams,' says Baker

SAN DIEGO — The five-year relationship between Barry Bonds and Jeff Kent is too complex to yield the simple conclusion that they hate each other. They are not friends, nor even friendly, but at times they have sworn they respect each other.

On the other hand, there is no question that sometimes they can't stomach being near each other.

One of those moments arrived Tuesday night at Qualcomm Stadium, early in the Giants' 10-7 loss to the San Diego Padres. Bonds and Kent engaged in a screaming and shoving match in the Giants' dugout and had to be separated. At one point Bonds pushed Kent against the wall.

The fight, which also involved third baseman David Bell and included manager Dusty Baker yelling at Kent, was captured on camera. Thus, while the Giants were coming back from a 5-0 deficit to take a 7-5 lead, only to lose when the Padres pounded Felix Rodriguez in a five-run seventh, the nation got to see the 2000 and 2001 National League Most Valuable Players go at each other.

Bonds refused to comment, while Kent called the episode "no big deal." Kent revealed that he has had several physical altercations with Bonds since they became teammates in 1997.

"Add this to the half-dozen times we've done it before," said Kent, who said the fight actually helped the Giants get off the mat after they fell behind 5-0 after two innings. In the inning immediately after the altercation, Bonds hit a three-run homer, and Kent homered in the sixth.

Kent also revealed that he once hit a grand slam right after sparring with Bonds.

"Barry and I have played together for five years," Kent said. "If there is any dislike I don't think we'd be playing together. So much has been made (of) the relationship between Barry and me. We have a good relationship. We have a working relationship that I think works well on the field.

"I think we do a lot of good things together on the field for this team that benefit him and benefit me. I think if you guys try to create a dysfunctional relationship, that's a farce too, because that's not true."

The fight occurred after the Padres scored four runs in the second to take a 5-0 lead. The pivotal play was a slow one-out chopper to Bell, who tried to force Wiki Gonzalez at second base. Kent overran the bag before taking the throw, and everybody was safe.

Kent said he was yelling at Bell to get the out at first, which would have meant two out, a runner at second and pitcher Kevin Pickford batting. Bell said he thought the best play was at second.

According to witnesses, once the inning ended Bell and Kent started yelling at each other in the dugout.

"David Bell and Jeff Kent started throwing F-bombs back and forth, Barry stuck up for David Bell. Jeff Kent then started going 'F— you' to Bonds, according to a fan who provided only his first name, Scott. He was sitting in small section of field-level seats that are practically inside the Giants' dugout. There is a clear view of the entire dugout from those seats.

A groundskeeper standing nearby provided a similar account to an Associated Press photographer. Bell declined to comment, saying, "I'd rather not. It's something that just happened on our team."

The fan said Bonds and Kent started yelling at each other before Bonds shoved Kent. Baker pulled Kent away and head trainer Stan Conte restrained Bonds. Baker then started yelling at Kent, later saying the second baseman said something the manager did not like.

Scott, the fan, said Kent yelled that he wanted off the team and Baker responded, "Don't you ever talk that way to me."

Another account had Kent telling Baker that this was Bonds' team anyway. Kent would not discuss anything that he said in the dugout, and Baker sniffed, "How are you going to believe what some fan said?"

Baker, like any manager, has to deal with these things all the time. Almost a

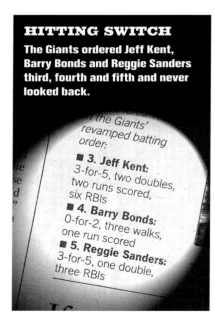

HITTING SWITCH

The Giants ordered Jeff Kent, Barry Bonds and Reggie Sanders third, fourth and fifth and never looked back.

...ared the Giants' revamped batting order:

■ **3. Jeff Kent:** 3-for-5, two doubles, two runs scored, six RBIs

■ **4. Barry Bonds:** 0-for-2, three walks, one run scored

■ **5. Reggie Sanders:** 3-for-5, one double, three RBIs

ear ago in the same dugout, Armando ios and Rich Aurilia went at each ther.

"It ain't a problem," Baker said. "I ent through the same thing in L.A. ith a couple of guys. Now we see each ther and we're partners. Usually this appens on good teams. Bad teams alays get along."

Baker further suggested the relationhip between Bonds and Kent is better han most people think.

"One thing's for sure," Baker said. They've helped each other, and they're ore similar than most people realize."

Remarkably, less than 10 minutes afer Bonds and Kent shoved each other, hey high-fived each other as Bonds rossed the plate after his three-run omer in the third.

"It happens in your job, too," Baker said. "I've seen sportswriters nearly come to blows in my office. The main thing is we lost the game. We didn't play a very good game."

Indeed, Ramon Martinez bobbled a double-play ball leading to the Padres' first run, and the Bell-Kent play fueled another four-run rally. After the Giants took a 7-5 lead in the seventh on a two-run Reggie Sanders single and a pinch RBI single by J.T. Snow, the Padres retook the lead in the bottom of the seventh after Rodriguez relieved Chad Zerbe with a man on first and one out.

Rodriguez walked Ron Gant after having him down 0-2, threw a wild pitch, then allowed an RBI single by Deivi Cruz, a fielder's choice that scored

a run and RBI singles by Julius Matos and Eugene Kingsale. The fifth run scored on a double steal.

The result was a bitter defeat that completed the San Diego half of this odd home-and-home series, sending the Giants home fractured as a family and reeling after losing a game they felt they had won.

When asked if the dugout brawl might ignite the Giants, Bell said, "It could. It depends on the character of the team."

Said Kent: "We had an emotional day both on the field and off. Teams have those. Add that to the half-dozen or dozen times this team has done that. It's a nonissue. It's something you keep inhouse. It's visible today, but something that's not a big deal." ◆

Giants manager Dusty Baker says the relationship between his star sluggers is better than most people think. Above, Jeff Kent (left) congratulates Barry Bonds on a home run.

Still waiting to hit stride

High expectations at the break rely on consistency and more 'career years'

JULY 11, 2002

By Henry Schulman
CHRONICLE STAFF WRITER

Ask not what the front office can do for the Giants. Ask what the Giants can do for themselves.

General manager Brian Sabean's reputation as one of the sneakiest used-car salesman on the lot has fostered renewed expectations that he can punch a few numbers on his cell phone and conjure up a deal that will push the Giants to a National League West title.

Sabean has no such expectations. He has fielded a $74 million team, and though he will hustle the next three weeks to find players who can help the cause, Sabean believes the 25 Giants who open the second half against Colorado at Pacific Bell Park tonight can and should do the job.

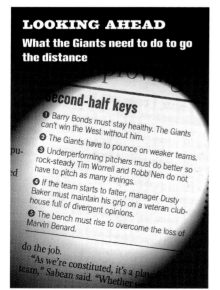

LOOKING AHEAD

What the Giants need to do to go the distance

Second-half keys

❶ Barry Bonds must stay healthy. The Giants can't win the West without him.

❷ The Giants have to pounce on weaker teams.

❸ Underperforming pitchers must do better so rock-steady Tim Worrell and Robb Nen do not have to pitch as many innings.

❹ If the team starts to falter, manager Dusty Baker must maintain his grip on a veteran clubhouse full of divergent opinions.

❺ The bench must rise to overcome the loss of Marvin Benard.

do the job.

"As we're constituted, it's a playoff team," Sabean said. "Whether

"As we're constituted, it's a playoff team," Sabean said. "Whether we become a playoff team is really going to depend on how well we play as well as what happens to the two teams in front of us, which we can't control when we're not playing them.

"I think it's obvious we can play better. We've shown signs of that. It's just a matter of how consistent we can be, including starting the second half. It's obvious some guys who've had subpar first halves are going to have to come through for us."

Sabean gets no arguments from downstairs.

"I think there is still some work to be done," outfielder Reggie Sanders said. "In order to win, everybody has to have career years, pretty much. That's basically what happened with the Diamondbacks last year. Everybody was having great years, so therefore it made everybody else's job a little bit easier."

Said shortstop Rich Aurilia, whose elbow surgery marred his first half: "In the beginning, our pitching carried us, and in a stretch of four, five games, our offense carried us. We haven't really put it together yet. I think the most we won in a row was seven games. We played well, but sporadically.

"If you'd have told us in the first half we'd be nine, 10 games over .500, we'd have said, 'Great.' But in here it's kind of a letdown because we know we could have played a lot better."

The Giants actually finished the first half 11 games over .500, at 49-38, a record forged with a great early run by the starters, a dominating performance by the bullpen, solid defense, another record-threatening season from Barry Bonds and a late charge by Jeff Kent.

On the flip side, they held themselves back with a maddening inability to hit

in the clutch in close games, resulting in a 20-19 record in games decided by one or two runs. The rotation, which consistently gave manager Dusty Baker six or seven innings a game early in the season, tuckered out. The starters took a 32-31 record into the break, allowing a 6.02 ERA over the last 14 games.

History is on the Giants' side. They have been good closers the past two seasons with an NL-best 95-56 second-half record.

They will be challenged early. After four games against the woeful Rockies, the Giants play 14 against the Dodgers and Cardinals, the first-place teams in the West and Central divisions, respectively, and the Arizona Diamondbacks.

However, the August schedule is like a visit to the Hostess Cupcake factory, full of the Phillies, Pirates, Cubs, Marlins and Mets. The Giants have faltered often in the first half against teams with inferior records.

"We've shown signs of being able to play series like the Yankees series, and we've shown signs of not being able to take care of business, like the Baltimore

Rising to the preseason expectations w require better play on defense including David Bell, above, and better production from hitters such as J.T. Snow, right, sliding ahead of Barry Bonds.

years are Barry and Benito (Santiago). Jeff is approaching it. David Bell and (Tsuyoshi) Shinjo have gotten less than how they've hit the ball. Felix is just approaching Felix right now. A lot of guys are on the come."

And, while praising the Dodgers for their surprising first half, Baker figures they are due for some struggles, saying, "On the other teams, a lot of guys are as good as they're going to get. It's hard to stay as good as you're going to get."

The 2002 Giants can't overwhelm opponents with long rallies fueled by singles and doubles. They rely on home runs and lead the NL with 107. They also lean on a pitching staff that ranks fourth in the league in ERA (3.80) and a defense that has turned a league-best 100 double plays.

Baker, ever the optimist, is betting the pieces will come together.

"I still think it's our year," he said. "It's going to work its way out. You get a six- or seven-game winning streak and bam! You know it's going to come. Here we are 11 games over .500 and we haven't hit our stride." ◆

:ries," Sabean said. "You're not going) have any more 'mulligans' in the sec- nd half. You're going to have to put .way teams you can put away and hope- ally hold your own in your own divi- on and play around .500 on the road."

Baker insists the Giants will get bet- r. He sees Felix Rodriguez's 5.55 ERA s an aberration. He is frustrated by Li-

van Hernandez's attitude and perform- ance (6-10, 4.94 ERA) but hopeful he will rebound like last year, when he was 6-11, 6.07 in the first half, 7-4, 4.20 in the second half.

"How many guys are close to their average years if you break it down at the half?" Baker said. "Is Richie? Is Reggie? The only guys who are having average

Hurtin' hammies

Bumps, pulls and bruises strain team's lineup as 3-4-5 hitters warm the bench

JULY 23, 2002

Henry Schulman
CHRONICLE STAFF WRITER

St. Louis closer Jason Isringhausen reads the papers. He knows Barry Bonds is hurt. Isringhausen also knows baseball, which means he knew he was not going to fly through the ninth inning Monday night without seeing Bonds, bad hamstring or not.

Sure enough, with St. Louis leading by two runs, Ramon Martinez on second base and Rich Aurilia at the plate, Bonds stepped out of the dugout as the Pacific Bell Park crowd roared.

When Aurilia struck out for the second out, Bonds went to bat with one purpose: tying the game with a home run. He wasn't going to leg out a double.

Bonds built the count to 3-2. Then Isringhausen dropped the hammer on Bonds, a beauty of a curveball. Bonds swung over it, ending a 5-3 Cardinals victory over a Giants team that opened the night without Bonds and without a suddenly hobbled Jeff Kent, then lost Reggie Sanders in the sixth inning to a tight hamstring.

As the game waned, head trainer Stan Conte told manager Dusty Baker that Bonds was available to pinch-hit. When the right time came, Bonds was there, just three nights after hurting himself in Los Angeles.

"Sometimes you've got to do what you've got to do," Baker said. "I figured they'd pitch to him because Izzy's been tough on him. We took a shot, and he struck him out on a good pitch."

Bonds has not gotten a hit off Isringhausen. He's 0-for-11, so there was no chance the former A's stopper was going to throw four wide ones to Bonds to bring Benito Santiago to the plate as the potential winning run.

"It's not my style," Isringhausen said. "I'm not going to nitpick. I'm going to throw strikes. I don't want to walk him. But I wasn't going to give him a 3-2 shot down the middle either. I've got a base open. I knew he had a bad leg. They were going to pinch-run for him anyway if he walked. I'd much rather have that than give him a shot down the middle and have him knock it into the water."

Hence, the full-count curveball.

"You still don't want him up there in that situation. Bottom line," Isringhausen said.

The Giants were so shorthanded because of illness and injuries that Martinez, who had three hits starting in place of Kent, would have moved to left field had Bonds put one into the drink.

Kent was scratched with what was termed a mild strain of the left calf. Baker said before the game that Kent hadn't fully healed after being hit by a pitch. He was drilled by Colorado's Justin Speier on July 11.

Kent told Baker he was sore before the game, and the manager did not want to take a chance with baseball's hottest hitter over the past six weeks.

"For him to mention it to me it's got to mean something," Baker said. Kent pinch-hit in the eighth and struck out as well.

Sanders left the game after ground-

The Giants were so shorthanded because of illness and injuries that Martinez, who had three hits starting in place of Kent, would have moved to left field had Bonds put one into the drink.

ing into a force to end the fifth inning. His status was uncertain.

Even with their 3-4-5 hitters out, the Giants nearly pulled off another dramatic win. They tied the game 3-3 on David Bell's two-run homer in the eighth inning off Steve Kline.

The Cardinals, though, managed a rare rally off setup man Tim Worrell in the ninth. Placido Polanco doubled, and after Worrell walked Jim Edmonds intentionally — Edmonds had hit a two-run homer off Livan Hernandez in the fifth — he walked Albert Pujols on four pitches to load the bases.

Robb Nen was asked to conjure another great escape, but he couldn't do it. After Tino Martinez popped out, Edgar Renteria doubled home two runs off the right-field wall, the first runs charged to Worrell since May 29.

Afterward, Baker had no idea what kind of shape the Giants would be in for tonight's game against All-Star Matt Morris.

"I'm going to start making my lineup up in pencil," he said.

Bonds is not expected back in the lineup tonight, for he is not ready to sprint. He is also not ready to talk. When asked about his pinch-hitting appearance after Monday night's game, he said, "No comments, guys, there's nothing to talk about." ◆

Giants outfielder Reggie Sanders grimaces because of a tight hamstring as he gets picked off at first base, left, against the Dodgers. Three days earlier, Sanders tended to Barry Bonds in the outfield after the slugger pulled a hamstring in the 11th inning against Los Angeles.

600!

Historic smash on a balmy night lifts Bonds into elite corps of sluggers

AUG. 10, 2002

By Henry Schulman
CHRONICLE STAFF WRITER

I t was so funny hearing the talking TV heads say Barry Bonds was "still stuck on 599 home runs" after the past two games. He hit that odd-numbered homer against the Cubs on Tuesday night, and anyone with a lick of sense knew 600 was coming, and soon.

Of course Bonds would hit it at Pacific Bell Park. Of course he would hit it against the Pittsburgh Pirates, for whom he started this trek of power, this long hike toward Cooperstown, more than 16 years ago. The only question was whether the ball would disappear into the clear blue sky or the black of nightfall.

Bonds chose nightfall, a rare August evening when his fans could celebrate in shirt sleeves.

At 9:24 p.m., in the sixth inning of a game the Giants would lose 4-3, Bonds joined Hank Aaron, Babe Ruth and Willie Mays in baseball's most exclusive foursome. With two out and nobody on, he smashed a 2-1 pitch from Pittsburgh right-hander Kip Wells over the center-field wall for his 600th career home run.

Bonds became the first player to reach that plateau since Aaron did it on April 27, 1971, against Gaylord Perry of the Giants in Atlanta.

Only one thing could have made the feat more special for Bonds — had he been able to win the game when he batted in the eighth inning, against Scott Sauerbeck, with two out, two on and the Giants down by a run. But he grounded out to second baseman Pokey Reese, who was shifted into short right field.

Mike Williams shot the Giants down in the ninth, and they fell 7½ games out in the NL West and 1½ games out in the wild card.

Only Wells knows where he was trying to throw his 2-1 pitch to Bonds in the sixth. Lord knows Wells could not have meant to throw it where he did, right over the plate, at the knees, trying to protect a 4-2 lead.

That baseball had no chance.

With that sweet uppercut, so familiar in this place and in this game, Bonds crushed it 421 feet, just left of straight-away center. Center fielder Adam Hyzdu drifted back, a waste of energy. He fooled nobody, as the crack of the bat foretold where the ball would land.

Bonds took five backward steps toward first base, and when the ball cleared the wall he raised his left arm and began a trot only three other men have known.

Fireworks erupted over McCovey Cove. Sparklers shot from the home-run

tote board in right-center, as the number next to Bonds' name moved from 599 to 600.

When Bonds touched home plate, he pointed to the sky with both hands. He was alone, but not for long. His teammates filed out of the dugout, Reggie Sanders covering the point. Sanders hugged him, and then came the high fives, then a sweet walk to the dugout with his helmet doffed to the crowd.

Bonds pointed to his family, sitting near the Giants' dugout, including his father Bobby, a recovering cancer-surgery patient who nonetheless vowed to follow his son across the country if necessary to the historic home run. Barry saved his dad a trip to Atlanta in August. He's a good son.

There was no midgame ceremony planned, but Wells knew this was going to take awhile. As he threw a few warm-up tosses to catcher Jason Kendall, the fans beckoned Bonds for a curtain call. He emerged from the steps closest to home plate, waved and ducked back

Barry Bonds hits his 600th home run, right, against the Pittsburgh Pirates at Pacific Bell Park on August 9. Above father Bobby Bonds is congratulated b[y] fans as he holds the bat (wrappe[d] in white cloth) that hit the run.

CLIMBING THE LIST

Barry Bonds slugged past many of the game's greatest home run hitters to become No. 4 the list.

500 club

1. Hank Aaron	755
2. Babe Ruth	714
3. Willie Mays	660
4. Barry Bonds	600
5. Frank Robinson	586
6. Mark McGwire	583
7. Harmon Killebrew	573
8. Reggie Jackson	563
9. Mike Schmidt	548
10. Mickey Mantle	536
11. Jimmie Foxx	534
12. Willie McCovey	521
Ted Williams	521
14. Ernie Banks	

After Benito Santiago grounded out to end the sixth, Bonds waited momentarily before jogging to left. Wouldn't you need a moment to compose yourself?

down. That wouldn't do. As Bonds paced across the dugout the fans wanted more, and he gave them more, popping up from the other set of dugout stairs.

Pirates manager Lloyd McClendon popped out of his dugout to talk to his pitcher. This was, after all, a 4-3 game.

After Benito Santiago grounded out to end the sixth, Bonds waited momentarily before jogging to left. Wouldn't you need a moment to compose yourself?

When he finally took the walk, tipping his cap to the bleacher creatures, two workers unveiled a new "Barry Bonds 600" decal on the left-field fence, between the cartoon car and the 'Bonds Squad' sign.

As Jason Schmidt pitched the top of the seventh, the stadium was in a fog, not literally, of course. The air was warm and clear. The murmur from the home run still hung over the proceedings, important as they were in the larger scheme if not the moment.

This game was a pitching rematch from last Saturday at PNC Park, an 11-6 Giants victory in which Schmidt won his first game back in Pittsburgh and Bonds hit a three-run homer off Wells.

With the China Basin thermostat reading 78 degrees and the flags still at first pitch, the climate was right for home runs.

Sure enough, moments later, history. ◆

Barry Bonds beams and waves to the crowd and cameras during one of several curtain calls after hitting his 600th home run in the sixth inning. Only Hank Aaron, Babe Ruth and Willie Mays have reached the slugging milestone.

The world of Barry Bonds

Pure slugger changes the game, earns spot in mythical lineup of all-time greats

BRUCE JENKINS

Barry Bonds, below, relaxes in the clubhouse with a trainer a few days before hitting home run No. 600. At right, Bonds spends a quiet moment at home with his daughter, Aisha, and wife, Liz.

AUG. 12, 2002

Somehow, you can't imagine Jim Thome in the team photograph. Even Alex Rodriguez is a stretch. Ken Griffey, once a lock to shatter all records, stands in the background. It takes a wholly authentic figure — like Barry Bonds — to join the 600 club.

Nobody much cared about 600 homers when Babe Ruth dwarfed the achievements of all who had come before. Henry Aaron had sort of a temporary guest pass, on his way to greater things. But Willie Mays has been gloriously frozen at 660 career home runs for nearly 30 years. The number is so gaudy, in relation to all the great players below him, it doesn't sound like any third-place relegation. It sounds incredibly cool.

You don't just barge into Mays' house without proper credentials, and

that's why Bonds' inclusion seems so appropriate. Criticize his attitude, his loafing on the bases or his defensive limitations, but this is a man who accomplished something believed to be impossible: As a pure home-run hitter, with all of the aura and respect that measure a legend, Bonds has entered Ruth's class.

Aaron was the greatest line-drive hitter who ever lived. His best shots just happened to go out, and he never even cracked 50 in a season.

Mays was so much more than a home-run threat, one could not categorize him so simply. He was the best baserunner, had the most instinctive genius, threw with the most strength and accuracy, had the most weapons of demoralization.

With Bonds, however, we get Ruth. We get an idea of what it must have been like. It's all about homers with Bonds at

this stage of his life, and the undeniab[l] superiority a single ballplayer possesse[s] over everyone else.

Ruth had his contemporaries, grea[t] sluggers all: Jimmie Foxx, Lou Gehri[g] Hack Wilson, Hank Greenberg. But i[n] the court of public opinion, the[y] couldn't hold a candle to Ruth when [it] came to the act of home-run hitting, ho[w] his performances stirred emotions an[d] shattered all precedent.

Ruth changed the game. Hell, h[e] damn near invented it.

Bonds is operating under the heav[y] cloud of steroid accusations, and ther[e] are those who won't acknowledge h[is] 73-homer season — and entry into th[e] 600 Club — as legitimate. Bonds, Mar[k] McGwire, Sammy Sosa, whateve[r] comes in the future — all bunk, to hea[r] some people tell it. And that's regre[t] table, a tiresome argument as viewe[d] from this corner.

But all the same, Bonds has change[d] baseball.

Nobody walked Ruth, Mays o[r] Aaron intentionally with a five-run lea[d] two out and nobody on base in the sev[] enth inning, as Tampa Bay manager H[al] McRae did so hopelessly a few week[s] back. People like Willie McCovey an[d] Willie Stargell got some mighty tips o[f] the cap, but they weren't avoided lik[e] the plague every single time. It's a mi[nd]

cle when Bonds gets a middle-in pitch. When the count goes to 2-and-0, it's time to just give up and walk him. Such is the residue of outright fear.

Bonds has ruined the game, to be honest — or at least an alarming number of Giants games. It's not his fault, but the league-wide refusal to compete against Bonds is, while vaguely intelligent, plainly disgraceful.

Where does he rank on the all-time team, that mythical nine trotting onto the field of dreams? That's a tough one. If you ask me — and most likely you didn't — he's right there.

I always figured if you didn't go strictly by position, Ruth would be in right field, Mays in center and Aaron in left. I followed Aaron with a crazed passion from around 1958 on, and he's just the classiest great player I ever saw (don't ask how Joe DiMaggio, Mickey Mantle and Ty Cobb get left out; the issue is complicated enough already).

In the category of actual left fielders, no cheating, I always took Ted Williams, with a nod to the select few who played Hall of Fame defense.

For the all-around glove: Joe Rudi.

For holding somebody to a single on a shot down the line: Rickey Henderson in the early '80s. For a laser throw to cut someone down at the plate: Stargell, before his shoulder went bad. If you're in Fenway: Carl Yastrzemski. And don't forget that for pure two-way excellence, Dusty Baker was an MVP-caliber player for the great Dodger teams of the late '70s and early '80s. But never Bonds; not on defense. His arm never passed the accuracy test.

With all of that said, now it's the top of the first. I'm leading off with Pete Rose, at third base, just to get everybody riled. I've got Rose in his prime, singling sharply to center, then sliding headfirst into third on a single by my second baseman, Jackie Robinson.

It's always tempting to lead off with Mays, recalling that one All-Star Game when he christened the proceedings with a triple. If that didn't characterize National League ball in the Sixties, nothing did. But in reality, he must bat third. And Ruth, naturally, bats fourth.

The No. 5 hitter is definitely not Jeff Kent. It's none of the guys who followed a legend and couldn't cope. I want an-

other Ruth in the No. 5 slot, someone just as feared, a guy who gets one good pitch — out of 40, maybe — and smokes it out of the park.

So many options sound good: Williams, Gehrig, Frank Robinson, Stan Musial. But I'll take Bonds, at least for a couple of at-bats. If you've been a regular at Pac Bell Park in recent times, you know why.

There's an interesting passage from Bonds in "This Gracious Season," Josh Suchon's revealing book on Bonds' history-making assault. Referring to the combined accomplishments with his father, Bobby, he says, "You hear all this talk about Ken Griffey Jr. and his father, and the Ripkens. But they haven't done anything compared to us. We're in the history books, man, the first father-son to crack 30-30 (among many other feats). They never gave my dad the respect he deserves. Why should I believe things will be any different for me?"

There is a reason. It's because Barry Bonds split the television screen. There's the rest of the game on one side, then the Bonds side. Under the weight of genius, all trifles collapse. ◆

In a scene that evokes memories of the off-the-field life of another slugger, Babe Ruth, a group of children follow Barry Bonds on the way from the Giants clubhouse to his car after the game.

CHAPTER 4

TURNING POINTS

Lofton juices the Giants

Timely trade from Chicago gives S.F. another weapon in thick of wild-card battle

JULY 31, 2002

By Henry Schulman
CHRONICLE STAFF WRITER

The White Sox sure snookered the Giants, didn't they? San Francisco thought it was getting a leadoff hitter who would smack the ball around the infield and leg out singles, then steal his way around the bases.

So here comes Kenny Lofton, driving the second pitch he sees as a Giant over the left-field wall for a home run. Five innings later, he drives a ball into the gap in right-center for a triple.

Speed demon? Looks like the Giants got another power hitter.

Lofton's 24th leadoff homer sent the Giants rolling to a 10-3 rout of the Philadelphia Phillies at steamy, sticky Veterans Stadium. Once again, a Brian

HELP ON THE WAY

GM Brian Sabean has pulled off numerous midseason trades that propelled the Giants in the second half. Among the players he has picked up:

1997 — Pitchers Wilson Alvarez, Danny Darwin and Roberto Hernandez from White Sox

1998 — Outfielder Ellis Burks from Rockies

1999 — Pitcher Livan Hernandez from Marlins

2000 — Pitcher Doug Henry from Astros

2001 — First baseman Andres Galarraga from Rangers

2002 — Outfielder Kenny Lofton from White Sox

Sabean acquisition paid quick dividends, like Andres Galarraga last year and Ellis Burks in 1998.

"You never know when you make a trade, but it has kind of worked out that way since I've been here," winning pitcher Kirk Rueter said. Rueter beat Philadelphia when Burks homered in his second game as a Giant four years ago.

"As soon as we get a guy, he gets going and everyone follows," Rueter said after he allowed two runs in six innings. "I hope he'll start us on a nice run these last two months."

The important caveat: This was just one win against a team that just traded its best player, Scott Rolen. It lifted the Giants into a tie for the NL wild card with Los Angeles and moved them five games behind Arizona in the West.

After Lofton's homer, Tom Goodwin singled and scored on a J.T. Snow sacrifice fly, following a Jeff Kent single. The Giants chased Myers with a four-run fourth that began with a Kent double. Myers hit Snow before David Bell singled to load the bases for Reggie Sanders, who played for the first time in seven games.

Myers hit Sanders to force home a run before Yorvit Torrealba singled home two more to KO Myers. One out later, with the bases again loaded, Sanders scored for a 6-0 lead when Goodwin raced to first to stay out of an inning-ending double play.

After Lofton's one-out triple in the sixth, he showed off his speed when Goodwin bounced a ball to shortstop Jimmy Rollins, who was playing in. Lofton bolted for home and forced a wide throw from Rollins. The error moved Goodwin to second, and he scored on a Rich Aurilia single.

"That was a heck of a game right away. We needed it, especially against a

guy we've never seen before," manager Dusty Baker said.

The Giants were hoisted not only by Lofton's offense and enthusiasm — he led the postgame high-fives — but also by Sanders' return from a hamstring injury. He contributed an outstanding defensive play.

With Rueter leading 2-0 in the second, Mike Lieberthal singled with one out. Travis Lee then rapped a one-hop-

er off the right-field wall. Sanders calmly jogged to a spot, waited for the op and nailed Lee at second base. That mothered the rally, which ended with o runs.

"For real, I didn't think I had a hance," said Sanders, who marveled at Lofton's effect on the Giants in his first ame.

"Kenny creates havoc whenever he's n the lineup, because of his defense, be-

cause of his speed. To see him hit the home run, he was in awe of that. He's not known for hitting home runs. It was definitely a great start for him and us. A lot of times when you go to a new team it takes time to get adjusted. For him to start the way he did escalated us."

Lofton has been traded before, but never in midseason. He said that getting his first hit so quickly helped relieve some angst, which was not too bad to

begin with because he is not a total stranger in the Giants' clubhouse. J.T. Snow was a college teammate. Shawon Dunston and Tim Worrell played with him in Cleveland.

"There are some guys in here I already know," he said. "That makes it a lot more comfortable coming into a new situation, with guys I've played with before and guys I've known for a long time. That makes the transition easier." ◆

Kenny Lofton scores a run in his first game as a Giant. He also hit a home run and a triple in the win over Philadelphia.

Sabean questions, Giants respond

General manager challenged $74 million team to break out of losing streak

AUG. 20, 2002

By Henry Schulman
CHRONICLE STAFF WRITER

MIAMI — General manager Brian Sabean sat in his box at Pro Player Stadium, munching on popcorn at the start of Monday's game against Florida, and assessed the Giants at the tail end of a bad road trip.

"We're 17-18 since the break," he said. "We flirt anywhere between 10 and 14 games above .500 and we can't get on a roll. You look at the team statistics and you're fairly encouraged, but the bottom line is when you have stretches like this, you need a stopper.

"You need somebody to come out and pitch big for you, and we haven't had that, or a string of two-out base hits or somebody knocking in a run with a base hit instead of striking out."

Then, as if by executive fiat, the Giants filled Sabean's order by beating Florida 3-0 to snap a four-game losing streak.

Livan Hernandez pitched a five-hitter for his fourth career shutout and a lineup without Barry Bonds made enough hay out of five hits against former mate Julian Tavarez. Tom Goodwin, Jeff Kent and David Bell drove in the runs.

The victory was medicine for the mind, lightening the load of recrimination on the Giants' six-hour flight home after a 2-4-1 trip.

As manager Dusty Baker put it, "It seems dopey to go out there and shake hands until you haven't done it for a while. This feels great."

In the larger picture, this win merely raised the Giants' record since the All-Star break to .500, hardly the run expected of a team that ordinarily gets legs this time of year.

This trip was particularly frustrating, for after last Tuesday's victory over Greg Maddux, the Giants lost 1-0 to Atlanta the next night and then had a 3-1 lead with two out in the ninth the following night, only to arrive in Miami at dawn the following day after a 3-3 tie. Then came three straight losses against the sub-.500 Marlins.

"The maddening thing was we were a hit away from winning the 1-0 game, if we were able to play situational baseball, which we didn't, and we were a strike away from what we needed to do to close out another game on the road," Sabean said. "Part of you says don't panic. You have a sense of confidence, but we are running out of games."

Sabean made it clear his players should not expect another infusion of talent. His cell phone has not rung in three days.

With 39 games left and the Giants trailing wild-card leader Los Angeles by 3½ games, they need to make their move, pronto, and Sabean puts the onus squarely on the $74 million team he has fielded.

"The owner can't do any more, the general manager can't do any more, the manager can't do any more," he said. "The pieces are here. The guys who are accountable are the guys who are in uniform. I have complete faith that we are going to get it together. I just hope it's sooner or later before it's too late. I still believe we're a playoff team. Whether that turns out is going to be up to these guys."

Strong performances by third baseman David Bell, above, and pitcher Livan Hernandez (getting hug from catcher Benito Santiago) right, keyed the Giants attempt to get back into the West Division race in late August.

"There's no fire and brimstone needed. Who are you going to motivate? If they don't motivate themselves, we're in trouble. There are times when you have to have a shutout. There are times when you have to get a two-out hit. We go the longest time without either."

Until now.

Hernandez extended his scoreless streak to 15 innings and earned his first victory since July 12 and only his fourth since April 19. The difference in his past two starts is obvious: He's throwing more fastballs.

"I had more fun watching him pitch today. It was great," pitching coach Dave Righetti said. "He's got plenty of talent. When he uses that fastball, the sky's the limit."

So why has he waited so long to pitch like this?

"It's the age-old question of trusting your stuff, and sometimes thinking too much," Righetti said. "It's a real simple game, and simple people sometimes do real well in this game."

Hernandez was happy to throw a shutout in his hometown in front of his family, including his mother, Miriam, to whom he presented the game ball.

"I saw my mom in the stadium in 90-something-degree heat. I'm happy she was able to see me throw a shutout," he said. "All my friends are here screaming, 'Yeah, Livo! Let's go.' It feels good."

With Hernandez pitching like an Opening Day starter should, the Giants' chances of turning this thing around are greatly enhanced. ◆

Series spins Kent's view of future

Prolific second baseman faces decisions about free agency

OCT. 22, 2002

By John Shea
CHRONICLE STAFF WRITER

Three more nights. Three more games. Jeff Kent knows they could be his last at Pacific Bell Park as a Giant.

"Yeah. To be honest with you, I've been thinking about that for three weeks now, ever since we started in the playoffs," Kent said after Monday's World Series workout.

"You think about all the possibilities, but none of them have come true yet. We're still playing. It's very pleasing we're having this conversation in the World Series rather than when I'm out hunting in my camouflage or out riding motorcycles."

Always a motorcycle reference.

Next month, Kent will file for free agency, beginning a process that could leave the Giants without the only second baseman in history to collect 100 RBIs in six straight seasons.

The streak started the year he arrived from Cleveland in the Matt Williams trade and extended through this year with a bonus — a career-high 37 home runs.

Kent won't say he'll return. Or wants to return. That's part of the posturing game. Same for manager Dusty Baker. Kent did hint that the Giants' postseason run has made him think more about his personal ties to the organization than ever before.

"These playoffs and World Series have definitely thrown a wrinkle into my decision-making — a positive wrinkle — and everything is a possibility," Kent said. "You forge some emotional relationships in the playoffs, especially when you win, that have more weight than in the regular season."

Owner Peter Magowan says he wants to keep the nucleus intact, but he keeps saying he won't raise the payroll. Kent makes $6 million and won't return without a sizable raise. The high-rolling Dodgers are said to be interested, along with the Rockies and Phillies and maybe the Braves, but Atlanta's priorities are its own free agents, Greg Maddux and Tom Glavine.

With Kent, it's more than the consistently strong numbers — he's averaging .297, 29 homers and 115 RBIs as a Giant. It's also the extracurricular activity. And the outspokenness. Kent speaks his mind, and his bosses don't always appreciate it.

The first day at Pac Bell, he was critical of the Giants' new cream-colored home uniforms. Last month, he had unfavorable words for the ballpark, Magowan's pride and joy, describing it as "brutal." He meant the hitting conditions, but it didn't go unnoticed by Magowan, who has fired back at Kent more this year than in the past.

Kent's spring-training caper — "breaks wrist in truck-washing accident" became "breaks wrist in motorcycle accident" — didn't sit well with club officials, and his slow start made things worse. Once he began hitting, he was fine again, at least until last month's ballpark analysis.

"Peter's super-sensitive about that," Kent said. "My comment about the ballpark was about reality, the fact it's not a hitter's ballpark. That doesn't damage Pac Bell. This is a beautiful ballpark, but not a hitter's ballpark. It's cold and it's windy. But it's got nothing to do with me not liking it. Hell, I was hitting .320 here when I made the comment. I like it here. Peter's sensitive to that, and he shouldn't be."

Magowan said he wants to clear the

Jeff Kent and his son Hunter, above, have a little discussion during team practice. Right, Kent avoids Montreal's Brad Wilkerson during a double play.

KENT BY THE NUMBERS

The second baseman's most prolific years have been with the Giants

Season	TM	G	AB	R	H	2B	3B	HR	RBI	BB	SO	AVG	SLG
1992	Tor	65	192	36	46	13	1	8	35	20	47	.240	.443
1992	NYM	37	113	16	27	8	1	3	15	7	29	.239	.407
1993	NYM	140	496	65	134	24	0	21	80	30	88	.270	.446
1994	NYM	107	415	53	121	24	5	14	68	23	84	.292	.475
1995	NYM	125	472	65	131	22	3	20	65	29	89	.278	.464
1996	NYM	89	335	45	97	20	1	9	39	21	56	.290	.436
1996	Cle	39	102	16	27	7	0	3	16	10	22	.265	.422
1997	SF	155	580	90	145	38	2	29	121	48	133	.250	.472
1998	SF	137	526	94	156	37	3	31	128	48	110	.297	.555
1999	SF	138	511	86	148	40	2	23	101	61	112	.290	.511
2000	SF	159	587	114	196	41	7	33	125	90	107	.334	.596
2001	SF	159	607	84	181	49	6	22	106	65	96	.298	.507
2002	SF	152	623	102	195	42	2	37	108	52	101	.313	.565

r with Kent after the World Series. ent should take a number. Magowan ants to clear the air with Baker, too.

"You sit down for a clear-the-air ses- on, and sometimes you muddy the r," Magowan said. "I don't want to istract Jeff from what he's doing right ow, which is contributing to the team. m sure he said some things he wishes e could take back. But what he says is ot really as important as how he plays. e's the best offensive second baseman probably 50 years."

In the end, that's more important an how he broke his wrist. Anyway, Magowan added this kicker: "We'd love have him back."

Baker is still waiting for such an en- orsement.

Leave it to Shawon Dunston to give — to everybody. Dunston, 39, also is cing the possibility of his last three ames at Pac Bell. The difference is, unston also is facing the possibility of retirement.

"I think the Giants' priority should be to sign Brian Sabean, Dusty Baker and Jeff Kent, and the rest of us are in the background," Dunston said. "All three together. Not one ahead of the other. They mean a lot to the organiza- tion, just as much as Barry (Bonds). Barry can't get here all by himself.

"I see Dusty managing the Giants next year. I'm not psychic, but he's sup- posed to stay here, and I hope he does. Everybody loves Dusty. He's the most popular player on the Giants. Not Barry. In introductions, Dusty gets the biggest cheer.

"Jeff's arguably our MVP, as impor- tant as Barry. If Barry's first, Jeff's sec- ond — a minute behind Barry. Jeff's out- standing. They need to sign all three. If one leaves, it'll hurt. Let everybody else leave."

Three more nights. Three more games. ◆

Road trip goes right

Giants revel in good fortune, big wins on long stretch away from home

AUG. 29, 2002

By Ron Kroichick
CHRONICLE STAFF WRITER

August's successful road trip relied in part on heavy hitting by Jeff Kent and Barry Bonds, opposite page, as well as efficient pitching – and some solid hitting – by Giants starting pitcher Russ Ortiz, below.

DENVER — This is not quite an epic, A's-like joyride into the record books. The Giants are still rolling merrily along, smashing home runs and pitching well and pocketing wins on a near-daily basis.

Or put another way: This is not an ideal time for labor strife to get in the way.

Wednesday night's 9-1 romp over Colorado gave the Giants eight victories in their past 10 games. Russ Ortiz threw eight shutout innings, allowing the bullpen welcome rest as it heads into today's series finale and (possibly) this weekend's three-game set in Arizona.

Ortiz was a model of efficiency in pushing the Giants a season-best 16 games over .500 (74-58). Rockies hitters spent most of the night trudging back to the dugout in frustration, often taking shattered bats with them.

Giants hitters mostly shattered incoming pitches. Jeff Kent, Barry Bonds and Benito Santiago each hit a solo home run.

Every starter but Rich Aurilia collected at least one hit. Ortiz had two RBIs himself.

Ortiz nearly completed San Francisco's first shutout in 46 games in Denver, covering two years at Mile High Stadium and eight at Coors Field. But with his team comfortably ahead and his pitch count at 119, Ortiz gave way to Scott Eyre in the ninth. The Rockies scored off Eyre to avert the shutout.

"I would have liked to pitch the ninth, but I realized I had a lot of pitches," Ortiz said. "There's no need to push it and have me throw 140 pitches."

Ortiz adapted to the altitude of Denver, where curveballs do not break as sharply as they do elsewhere. Pitching coach Dave Righetti estimated that Ortiz threw only five or six curves, probably one-third of his customary total.

Instead, he leaned on his slider to complement a howling fastball. The radar gun clocked Ortiz's fastball in the 92-to-93 miles per hour range all night, Righetti said.

"Russ was relaxed when he got in trouble," Righetti said. "That may be as good as he can pitch."

Said Ortiz, "My timing was there pretty much the whole game. I was able to let it loose and hit my spots."

Ortiz struck out eight and repeatedly

pitched his way out of budding Rocki threats. Most notably, he retired Tod Helton, Greg Norton and Jack Cust t escape a second-and-third, no-out ja in the fourth. Then, in the fifth, he froz Larry Walker with a full-count fastba to leave the bases loaded.

Meantime, the Giants pounced o Colorado starter Jason Jennings, a l gitimate candidate for Rookie of th Year. Jennings brought a 15-5 recor into the game, including 9-1 at th pitching graveyard known as Coor Field.

Jennings also had won six consecu tive decisions. He was 3-0 in four star this season against the Giants. In othe words, he was absolutely cruising, th closest thing to an ace in Colorado' crazy baseball world.

Well, not so fast.

Jensen quickly relinquished first-in ning home runs to Kent and Bonds, th second time in two nights (and all sea son) they have hit back-to-back homers

Kent launched No. 31 deep into th

ft-field seats, a no-doubt-about-it last. Bonds lifted No. 39 barely into the ft-field seats, an opposite-field Coors ield special. That set the tone for a night f steady production from San Fran- isco's lineup.

"Jennings is a good pitcher," Kent aid. "He might have looked a little red. He's a rookie and he's pitched a lot this year."

Rookies and veterans, righties and lefties — none of it matters to Bonds. He had three more hits, giving him these numbers in the series: 9-for-12, four homers, two doubles, five RBIs.

Bonds is now hitting .371 for the sea- son, giving him a suddenly sizable lead over Walker (.357).

Bonds also won over another oppo- nent in Rockies reliever Kent Mercker. He had stymied Bonds throughout his career, holding him without a home run in 30 at-bats — until Bonds creamed a changeup for his third and final homer Tuesday night.

"That guy is not human, he really isn't," Mercker said. ◆

Diversity on the diamond

Team of many nations reflects the city it represents

OCT. 19, 2002

When Giants manager Dusty Baker needs to give instructions to his back-up center fielder in the midst of a game, he punches four numbers on the phone in the dugout. It rings in the video room of the Giants clubhouse.

Katsunori Kojina, known to all as KK, picks up the phone. Then he flies out the door, down the stairs, past the indoor batting cage and up the 10 or so steps to the far corner of the dugout. There, he listens to Baker's instructions then quickly translates them to Tsuyoshi Shinjo in Japanese.

It's the baseball equivalent of a shopkeeper in Chinatown or the Mission summoning her daughter from a back room to translate a customer's request. In other words, it is a dance played out all over San Francisco every day, the bridging of language and the braiding of cultures in such a way that they intersect but remain distinct.

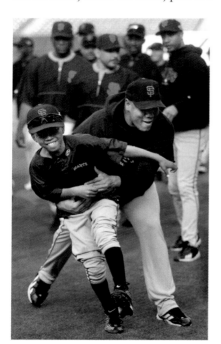

JOAN RYAN

That's what you'll find in the Giants clubhouse.

The National League Champion Giants hail from seven countries and three continents, which is not unusual in baseball today. But because San Francisco is such a melting pot, the multicultural Giants reflect their city more closely than most teams.

Before and after games, salsa often thrums through the clubhouse speakers as Giants players in the so-called "Latin Quarter" of the room move to the music as they dress by their lockers.

The Latin Quarter takes up the far right side of the clubhouse and comprises the lockers of Livan Hernandez from Cuba, Benito Santiago from Puerto Rico, Ramon Martinez, Pedro Feliz and Manny Aybar from the Dominican Republic, Marvin Benard from Nicaragua and Yorvit Torrealba from Venezuela. A few lockers away is Felix Rodriguez from the Dominican Republic.

On a nearby table, Benard sometimes spreads out *carne asada*, rice and beans and plantains from Las Tinajas, the Nicaraguan restaurant on Mission Street that has been a hub for Latin ballplayers for years.

"We're always trying to stuff Latin food into Shinjo," Benard says. "We don't think he eats enough."

It is no coincidence that Shinjo's locker is next to the Latin Quarter. The Latin players took him under their wing when he arrived last spring from the New York Mets.

"They all share of feeling of being foreigners," says KK, Shinjo's interpreter and close friend. It was KK who carried a rice cooker to road games early in the season so Shinjo's wife could make rice balls for some carbo-loading before games.

Language is still a barrier for Shinjo, though most of the baseball lingo is the same in English and Japanese. Shinjo apparently understands more English and Spanish than he can speak, though he has mastered greetings and essential words. And he can swear effectively in both languages ("men's words," as KK politely puts it). Shinjo knows he can crack up his teammates with an exuberant "Wassup, mother—!"

Giants outfielder Reggie Sanders has his own theory about why Shinjo hooked up with the Latin players. "They have a lot more fun than the American players," he said.

At a game this season in Chicago, center field fans tossed quarters and other objects at Benard, chanting "Mar-vin sucks! Mar-vin sucks!" When Benard complained about the flying objects to the umpire, the taunting grew louder. After the game, the team bus was quiet as it pulled away from Wrigley Field. Then from the back row, Shinjo began to chant. "Ma-vin sucks! Ma-vin sucks!" Everyone, including Benard,

Felix Rodriquez, above (second from right), of the Dominican Republic and Livan Hernandez far left, of Cuba are among a host of Giants from Latin American countries. Tsuyoshi Shinjo, top, gets his marching orders from Dusty Baker through an interpreter.

roke out laughing.

But some cultural differences still pop
p. After the playoff victory in Atlanta
his month, the Latin players led the
lubhouse celebration with Hernandez
howing Baker some hip-swiveling
noves and Aybar dancing with a bottle
f champagne in his back pocket.
hinjo, as outgoing and fun-loving as he
, ducked into the laundry room and
rank a few beers with KK. This wasn't
vhat he was accustomed to. In Japan,
eams celebrate at the hotel.

The Giants front office has had to ad-
ust to the growing number of foreign
layers and fans. The seven Japanese
eat writers sent to track Shinjo's every
nove this season immediately doubled
he size of the Giants' traveling press
orps and required that the team hire a
nedia relations coordinator who speaks
apanese.

Another coordinator, from Colom-
bia, has been handling all the Spanish-
speaking media for 10 years. The team
has a special phone line for the 12 Span-
ish-language newspapers in the Bay
Area that delivers a daily update on Giants news. There is a phone line just for
Spanish-speaking fans, too (972-2454).

Though they come from five different countries, the Latin players on the
Giants feel a fierce sense of solidarity.
"We are different countries but one
blood," Hernandez said.

Said Benard, "We all come from the
same hole. We come from nothing.
When we get to the big leagues, we don't
forget where we came from. All we have
is each other."

In the community relations depart-
ment, a Mexican American woman con-
nects the Latin players to health fairs and
school events and baseball clinics for the

city's Spanish-speaking community.
Santiago read aloud "Clifford the Big
Red Dog" at a neighborhood center in
the Mission. He asked the children questions about the story and had them answer in both Spanish and English, em-
phasizing the importance of speaking
both languages well.

"Doing something for the Latin community in San Francisco is very important for the Latin players," Hernandez
said.

Manager Dusty Baker doesn't speak
much Japanese, but he is fluent in Spanish. "On my staff I've got coaches who
are Cuban, Polish, French and three
black guys," Baker said. "If a player
can't find somebody to talk to, he's in
trouble."

And if a fan can't find a player to
root for, he or she isn't looking hard
enough. ◆

CHAPTER 5

STRETCH RUN

The rivalry

Giants' experience is the edge in race against old nemesis Dodgers

SEPT. 3, 2002

Henry Schulman
CHRONICLE STAFF WRITER

Eric Gagne of the Dodgers is one of the best closers in baseball this year, but Robb Nen has something over Gagne: a World Series ring.

Nen has pitched in meaningful September games in each of the past four seasons for the Giants. Gagne has not sniffed the playoffs.

Jeff Kent has the same edge over Dodgers second baseman Mark Grudzielanek, as does David Bell over Adrian Beltre, Rich Aurilia over Alex Cora and Cesar Izturis, and Reggie Sanders over Shawn Green.

With four weeks left in the regular season, the Dodgers and Giants are heading for a possible showdown for the National League wild card. Though Los Angeles leads in the standings, Giants manager Dusty Baker can cling to his team's edge in stretch-drive experience.

"It's not the determining factor of whether you're going to be successful or not, but it gives you an advantage," Kent said.

Indeed, a lack of pressure experience did not hold back the baby Oakland A's in 2000 as they won the American League West and took the New York Yankees to five games in their Division Series. Also, owning a World Series ring will not make Nen a better closer than Gagne over the last four weeks. Nen has blown five saves in the past month and would be the first to admit he must start making his pitches to help the Giants pass the Dodgers. On the other hand, Nen has felt the heat of the klieg lights in September and October, and that counts for something.

TO THE RESCUE

Closer Robb Nen is 11th on the all-time saves list with 314. Here are his totals with the Giants:

Year	Saves
1998	40
1999	37
2000	41
2001	45
2002	43
Total	**206**

"Everybody realizes what it takes to get there, and I think everybody who's been there has the desire to go back and go farther," Nen said. "The pressure of being there is great, but it's easier to deal with. You know what to expect."

While the Giants have won two NL West titles and been entwined in division or wild-card races every year since 1997, the Dodgers have not reached the postseason since 1996. They insinuated themselves into the NL West race early last September but faded quickly.

The Dodgers are not bereft of October experience. Marquis Grissom, Kevin Brown and Brian Jordan, for instance, have played in six World Series among them. Nevertheless, the Giants have more players who have been in the thick of things more recently.

Beer-quaffing friends could argue past closing time whether that makes any difference, or which team is hungrier, but there is little doubt the Giants' early playoff exits in 1997 and 2000, and their wild-card play-in loss to the Cubs in 1998, have them itching to go further.

"If you get to the playoffs a few times and you get eliminated, the desire gets more and more and you want to work harder to get there," Nen said.

The wealth of postseason experience on the Giants' roster is no accident. The front office looks for it, and the acquisitions of player such as Nen, Sanders, Kenny Lofton and Livan Hernandez were made with that in mind.

On the other hand, Giants starter Jason Schmidt is proof that lacking a fat stretch-drive resume is not necessarily a hindrance. He got his first real taste of meaningful September baseball last season and prospered.

"I had the time of my life," Schmidt said, insisting he never took the weight of the standings to the mound.

"The funny thing about it was, I didn't look at it that way. I went out and pitched," he said. "I didn't think, 'If I don't pitch good today, we're three games behind.' The biggest factor for me was being injured the year before. I was just so happy to be out there. Everything else didn't matter."

Therein lies the paradox of September baseball. It's stomach-churning for the fans, who die a thousand deaths with each turn on the field and get caffeine jitters whenever the out-of-town scoreboard changes. The players they cheer can't get that involved.

"Being able to control your emotions is the biggest key going into a race like that," Kent said. It's best, he added, to maintain a quiet confidence.

"If you walk out to the field not having faith that you're better than the next guy, there's no use in competing," he said. "You always have to believe. Whether it's true or not you have to have faith. Then you give it your best shot." ◆

Robb Nen celebrates his 300th career save, which came Aug. 6 against the Cubs. Nen's performance fueled the team's wild-card hopes.

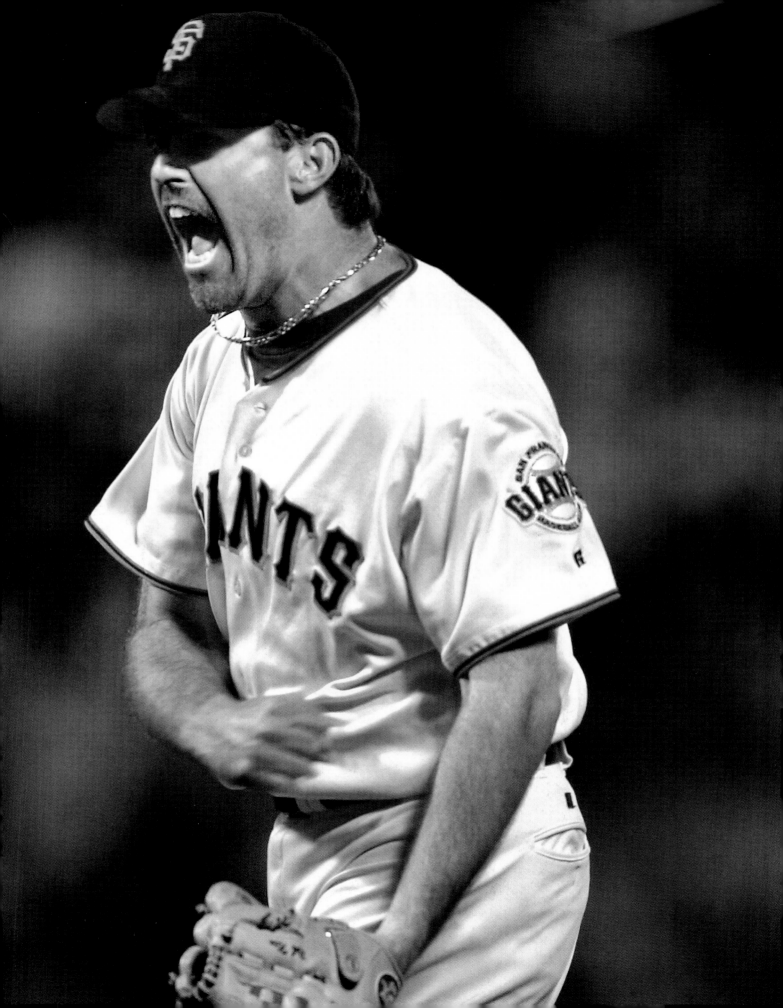

Baker plans a new chapter

San Francisco manager reflects, recharges after cancer surgery

MARCH 31, 2002

By Henry Schulman
CHRONICLE STAFF WRITER

Part I was Dusty the Student, a major league slugger with whiplike wrists who lashed 242 home runs over 19 seasons as he matured into manhood. Part II was Dusty the Teacher, a popular coach and manager aching to shepherd his San Francisco Giants to a championship.

Now there is Dusty the Cancer Survivor, whose drive to win is seasoned with a greater anticipation of the joys life might offer.

"There's going to be Dusty Part III," Dusty Baker says. "It's going to be a monster next few years, I think. Good stuff is waiting for me, probably better stuff than I could ever imagine."

He is not just projecting good things for the Giants, who open their 2002 season in Los Angeles on Tuesday. Three months after having his cancerous prostate removed, Baker understandably views life through refocused eyes.

He doesn't talk of living for today, but muses about leaving the hurly-burly of major league baseball behind and coaching his son, Darren, in Little League. That's eight or nine years down the pike. He daydreams aloud about reclining in a boat, day after summer day, casting his line into a lake in the Sierra foothills, an idyll that will have to wait.

"I've got some stuff to do," Baker says. "I've got some championships I have to win."

The season has yet to begin, but Baker is already 1-0. The victory was overcoming the toll the Dec. 17 operation took on his 52-year-old body and overseeing all 40 days of the Giants' spring training in Arizona. His doctors told him he might not return to full strength for a year. Joe Torre, the New York Yankees manager who underwent the same operation three years ago and helped guide Baker through the ordeal, advised him to slow down.

But Baker didn't miss a day. His coaches had to take the fungo bat out of his hands. His family and friends implored him to kick back. Baker did cut his nonbaseball schedule, trimming back his media time, saying no to many interview requests. His father, who flew down from Sacramento two weeks ago, added his voice to the nagging chorus.

"I got on him because I don't want him to do too much," Johnnie B. Baker Sr. says, "but he's got stamina up the ying-yang."

The elder Baker speaks with authority. Now 77, he was diagnosed with prostate cancer six years ago and beat it with radiation. Any man frets over his son's well-being, but Johnnie Baker had extra reason when he learned that prostate cancer was hereditary. He implored all four of his sons to get PSA tests, to keep on top of a disease that will strike 189,000 Americans this year, killing 30,000, according to the American Cancer Society.

Dusty Baker was diagnosed during a routine physical after the 2001 baseball season. His PSA numbers were too high, so doctors ordered a biopsy. He had one on his way to a pheasant hunt. The bad news came soon after.

"The first thing on my mind was, 'I don't believe it,' "Baker says. "You go through a period of denial. 'Hey, man,

Dusty Baker reveals a lighter side at spring training in Scottsdale, Arizona: gassing up his Indian motorcycle, above; mugging for a friend on the field, above left; and preparing for dinner, left, with his wife, Melissa

ot the kid. Not me.' The next thing you
ay is, 'OK, it's time to go to work. Let's
ce it head on and beat it.' Then you re-
ize you've got a lot to live for."

Baker's wife, Melissa, says he fought
ll the expected emotions, "the disbelief,
e 'why me?' because he felt he took
are of himself. He went to accepting.
hen Dusty, being the optimist, went
om accepting to knowing all was go-
g to be OK."

Baker had an all-star support group.
here was Bob Watson, a top assistant
 baseball Commissioner Bud Selig;
Vatson had prostate cancer and im-
lored Baker over the years to get tested.
here was Torre, who not only beat the
isease but returned to the dugout two
onths after his surgery and could tell

Baker what to expect. There was also
his father, of course.

Torre says he and Baker talked three
or four times before and after Baker's
surgery. "It's tough stuff," Torre says.
"You certainly want a security blanket
when you're involved in something like
that. The biggest thing you've got to get
over is the fact that we're all going to die
eventually, but being diagnosed with
cancer doesn't mean that's imminent."

Melissa Baker believes that seeing
Torre manage, watching Watson dole
out suspensions as baseball's discipline
chief, and enjoying time with his father
all have given Dusty more hope than
mere words could offer. They had the
disease. They survived. In fact, they have
thrived, so he can, too.

Melissa sees how well he takes care
of his body, stuffing a giant blender full
of fruit and liquefying a healthy breakfast each morning instead of downing
sausages and eggs.

She worries more about his mind
than his body. "The stress can drain
you," she says.

Anyone who knows baseball understands there is zero chance Baker can
avoid stress and angst unless he stays
home and lets someone else manage.

Giants fans can take this for granted:
Come Tuesday, Baker will don his No.
12 uniform, slip sweatbands on each
wrist, grab some toothpicks and assume
his customary game-watching position
on the top step of the dugout, ready to
start Dusty Part III. ◆

Happy ending?

Dusty and these Giants deserve more years together

OCT. 1, 2002

Let's say, for the sake of argument, that Dusty Baker is the best manager in baseball. It can't be too far off. With doubters lurking everywhere and a roster that often looked tired, he led the Giants to a 28-10 record down the stretch and into the postseason. Add his three Manager of the Year awards and his scintillating reputation around the game, and he's as good as they come.

Then say for certain that Barry Bonds is the best player in baseball, perhaps over the past 30 years. The evidence seems unassailable that he's the most feared hitter since Babe Ruth.

Now try to find two men, anywhere else in the playoffs, who are more on the spot. Jason Giambi? Curt Schilling? David Eckstein? Backups to injured starters? It's all small-time stuff compared with the Giants' duo. It's cruel, it's unfair, it's downright wrong — but it's reality as the Giants open their National League Division Series at Atlanta

BRUCE JENKINS

on Wednesday.

There's a very happy ending to all this. The Giants give it their best shot, taking it right down to Game 7 of the NLCS, maybe even battling into the World Series, and as the lockers empty that final day, Bonds approaches owner Peter Magowan with the very pointed suggestion that he rehire Baker. Dusty sits down with the owner, and the atmosphere is a little stuffy at first, but they come to acknowledge the beautiful partnership that includes Brian Sabean and his invaluable assistant, Ned Colletti. Come March, everyone's as fresh as a spring colt.

If it were only that easy. Some of the local critics see the Giants making a first-round exit. Bonds might see so few pitches to hit, he'll be lucky to get his career postseason average over .200. The tension between Baker and Magowan has become so palpable, it might be beyond repair. It's a New York, tabloid-press kind of climate, with disturbing issues churning beneath a smooth-sailing ship.

Right off the bat, Magowan should be ashamed of himself. If he thinks Baker gets too much credit, he hasn't properly assessed the mood around baseball. Magowan is universally praised for his role in keeping the Giants in San Francisco, in assuring fans of a contending team each year, of rounding up the private financing — damn near impossible in today's world — for building one of the best ballparks in America.

That's where it stops. There are no other avenues to acknowledge ownership.

Sabean builds the team, with a clever, consistent plan. Baker takes care of matters on the field. Magowan and Larry

Baer might have thrown out the firs pitches at the christening of Pacific Be Park, but they're not the baseball ge niuses of this outfit and never will be They should be delighted when peopl heap praise upon Sabean and, espe cially, Baker.

Magowan is a bottom-line guy, ruthless hard-liner in a crisis, and there nothing wrong with that. He's ha Baker for 10 years, with exactly on postseason victory to show for it. In th business world, that's curtains. Time fc a change. The issue of Baker's value though, is shaded with gray, calculabl beyond the numbers. There couldn't b more than a few teams around baseba that wouldn't take Baker in an instan

So don't mess up the dinner table wit

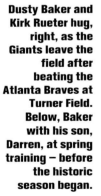

Dusty Baker and Kirk Rueter hug, right, as the Giants leave the field after beating the Atlanta Braves at Turner Field. Below, Baker with his son, Darren, at spring training — before the historic season began.

ame remarks like, "Whoever Brian de-
ides he wants as manager (assuming
abean stays) will be fine with me."
Don't pop off to a local magazine that
Baker might be getting too much recog-
ition. It's just not becoming.

Know this: Baker could be out of
ere, in his mind, right now. Criticism
nd disrespect don't roll off his back;
hey fester and grow. Even if the Giants
vin the whole thing, he could announce,
"It's been nice, everybody — I think it's
ime to move on." I distinctly remember
. scene in his office months ago when
Baker was discussing the annoying
barbs of second-guessing, and I asked
vhy it bothered him so much. "I'm tired,
nan," he said, with a penetrating look.
"Tired of it."

Remember, also, that Baker's
prostate cancer gave him a different out-
look on life. He's about time management, being in the right place, feeling
cool and comfortable. Sabean's genius
notwithstanding, it's hard to imagine
the Giants having a better shot next year,
with an older and more vulnerable roster, than they do right now. Long-term?
Dusty's already done that. If the climax
is less than satisfying, and Magowan
isn't in a shake-hands kind of mood,
Baker will make the call. He'll just van-
ish.

I'm trying to imagine that clubhouse
without Baker. Someone else coming to
grips with the fact that Bonds runs the
team, quite bitterly, in a world of his
own. Some other guy getting maximum

performances out of older, somewhat
jaded ballplayers, and realizing that
with Bonds around, there will never be
the kind of all-for-one spirit you see in
the Angels, A's and Cardinals.

It's a lot easier to imagine Bonds getting one good pitch to hit — maybe from
Greg Maddux in Game 2 — and crush-
ing a three-run homer that triggers a
whole new kind of postseason momentum for the Giants.

What Bonds needs now is a mistake,
at a time when no one will pitch to him.
One tailing fastball that gets a little too
much plate. He'll get high-fives all
around, and down in the dugout, he'll
make eye contact with Baker. Cherish
that moment if it comes. You'll remember these as the very best times. ◆

No substitute for a strong stretch

Big wins over old foes come at the perfect time

SEPT. 11, 2002

By Henry Schulman
CHRONICLE STAFF WRITER

Back in the day, the name Kevin Brown elicited a Pavlovian response from the Giants, marked by nervous tics, shivering, check-swing grounders and fruitless flailing at the plate.

The Brown who pitched for Los Angeles at Pacific Bell Park Tuesday night is a different man. These are different Giants. They have busted the shackles of mediocrity that bound them for much of the season and have begun to barrel through their opposition.

With a 5-2 victory over Brown and the Dodgers, the Giants have won five in a row, 13 of their past 16 and 17 of 23. They lead the wild-card race by a game and will make it two if they complete a three-game sweep today.

The hot streak has been fueled by victories over some good pitchers, a trend that was absent earlier in the season. Since Aug. 13, they have toppled Greg Maddux, Al Leiter, Javier Vazquez, Ja-

son Jennings, Mike Hampton twice (OK, he used to be good), Randy Johnson, Curt Schilling and Odalis Perez.

"We have a lot of confidence. You can see how the guys walk around and go about their business," said Benito Santiago, who produced the fifth run off Brown with a rare right-handed homer into the arcade in right. "We're winning now. There's nothing better than that. We've got to keep it on track."

The Dodgers have lost four in a row and begun to toss out the "we can't panic" quotes. As manager Jim Tracy said, "There's too much of the season left to look at it like this is the beginning of the end. It's not realistic."

It is also not realistic for the Giants to claim they now own Brown after beating him for the second time this year. This is a lost season for the right-hander after undergoing back surgery. That he is pitching at all is a testament to his fortitude, but his command and velocity were off.

GETTING WILD

The Giants are on the rise as the Dodgers begin to stumble

WILD CARD

Team	W	L	GB
	82	62	—
Giants	83	61	1
Dodgers	82	62	1
Astros	78	67	5½

▶ **Today's game:** Dodgers (Nomo 13-6) at Giants (Rueter 12-7), 12:30 p.m. ②

Dodger Shawn Green sets a collision course for Giants catcher Benito Santiago, right, in a game of the last home series between the two teams during a heated race for the wild-card spot in the National League. Left, Jeff Kent, held back by Barry Bonds, has some unkind words for a Dodger pitcher. Below right, Giants fans (from left) Mark Biagini, Mike Myers and Michael Hayes cheer during the opening of the Sept. 11 game against Los Angeles. An optimistic San Francisco fan, top, looking for a sweep against the Dodgers, waves the U.S. flag with a broom.

Barry Bonds hit a two-run single in the first inning after a leadoff single by Kenny Lofton, a Rich Aurilia bunt single and a Jeff Kent walk. The Giants took a 4-0 lead with a second-inning rally that began with a single by pitcher Jason Schmidt and included a disputed play at home on an Aurilia grounder to short. Schmidt was ruled safe even though he appeared to step on catcher Paul Lo Duca's glove and not the plate.

Brown settled into a groove and retired nine in a row until Santiago connected for the off-field homer, his first hit in 13 career at-bats against the pitcher.

The early run support smoothed the

rail for Schmidt, who contributed 7⅔ dominating innings. He allowed Shawn Green's 41st homer, but never let Los Angeles back into the game. He left to a standing ovation with a man on and two out in the eighth. Scott Eyre then fanned Green on a 3-2 slider to end the Dodgers' last threat, and Robb Nen pitched a 1-2-3 ninth for his 38th save.

"Scott Eyre came in and he was nasty to Shawn Green, one of the best hitters in the league. Then Robbie comes in and shuts them down. That puts a little something in their mind, that we've got this team," said Schmidt, who deflected much of the credit for his 11th win to his defense.

Schmidt overpowered hitters from the outset, in contrast with his last start against Arizona, when he gave up four first-inning runs. Santiago said when Schmidt showed him the Dodgers' lineup before Tuesday night's game, he told his pitcher to forget about the names and just throw.

"Sometimes good pitchers think too much," Santiago said. "This guy is one of the toughest right-handed pitchers I've ever caught. Sometimes you've got to plug it in. You've got to put some positive thoughts in his mind before he goes out and pitches." ◆

Time to deliver on six years of promise

Tough road ahead for team that has plenty to prove

SEPT. 30, 2002

By Henry Schulman
CHRONICLE STAFF WRITER

In 1997, they were the plucky over-achievers just happy to be in the playoffs, where they went three-and-out.

In 2000, they finished the regular season with the best record in the majors before the New York Mets finished them posthaste in the Division Series.

The Giants will attack the 2002 playoffs from a different angle, as the National League wild card, with a heightened sense of urgency born from the knowledge that all the good they did this year — indeed for the past six years — will mean squat if they exit the playoffs early again.

"As spontaneous and as wild as the celebration was last night, everybody knows what's at stake," general manager Brian Sabean said Sunday before the Giants ended the regular season with their eighth consecutive win, 7-0 over the Houston Astros.

"We've won a lot of games, but they

ROLLING INTO THE PLAYOFFS

The Giants finished with eight straight wins, closing their season 29-10.

Date	Score
9/20	Giants 5, Brewers 1
9/21	Giants 3, Brewers 1
9/22	Giants 3, Brewers 1
9/24	Giants 12, Padres 3
9/25	Giants 6, Padres 0
9/27	Giants 2, Astros 1
9/28	Giants 5, Astros 2
9/29	Giants 7, Astros 0

haven't necessarily meant too much, and they don't mean too much unless you get past the first round of the playoffs."

It won't be easy. The Giants will face a Braves team that has played in the Division Series all seven years of its existence and advanced six times with a combined record of 18-5.

Only one wild-card team, the 1997 Florida Marlins, has won a World Series, and the Marlins benefited from a bizarre first-round playoff format in which the Giants had the home-field "advantage" but started the best-of-five series with two games in Miami.

Even so, the Giants know how dangerous a wild-card team can be. After losing to the 1997 Marlins, the Giants were dumped in 2000 by the wild-card Mets, who a year earlier lost a heart-breaking National League Championship Series to the Braves.

Sabean sees value now in the Giants' failures of the past.

"Our loss in 2000, I really understood how it could happen if you look at the Mets," he said. "The year before, they were right on the brink and couldn't get past Atlanta. I think that made them hungry.

"The more recent experience you've had, good or bad, is going to fuel your fire. There are a lot of guys in here who are in the twilight of their careers, maybe their last round up. They're going to get their last breath."

Second baseman Jeff Kent won't be breathing his last, but this could be his

Giants swarm Robb Nen, right, as he gets the last out to beat Houston and secure a wild card spot in the playoffs. Above, Jeff Kent slides into third base safe for a triple in the third inning as Astros third baseman Geoff Blum waits for the throw. Left, Barry Bonds shares a moment with his son, Nikolai, after another home run.

last chance to sniff a title in San Francisco, where he matured into one of the game's elite hitters. The 2000 failure hurt Kent to the core.

After the Giants clinched the wild card Saturday, Kent expressed his belief they can overcome their past and navi-

gate the potholed path of a wild card seeking a title.

"Going into it, I think we feel good about our chances," he said. "The playoffs are totally different than the regular season. The regular season is a grind. The playoffs are a serious sprint. Whether we can sprint with all these other teams remains to be seen, but we're going into it with confidence and some emotion."

Because Jason Christiansen is on the 60-man disabled list, the club can replace him on the postseason roster with any pitcher who was in the organization on Aug. 31. Therefore, the Giants can draft Aaron Fultz, Manny Aybar or Troy Brohawn if they choose.

Whatever the Giants' makeup, they will ride into Atlanta as one of the hottest teams, having won their last eight games and 25 of their final 33, which guarantees them nothing.

As Baker pointed out several times this week, the 2000 Yankees finished the regular season with 15 losses in 18 games and still won the World Series.

In baseball terms, there is an eon between now and the first pitch of Game 1 on Wednesday.

"You have a lot of time to rest in-between," Barry Bonds said. "We get to rest until Wednesday. Is that going to put us out of sync because we've been in sync playing every day? Time will tell. On Wednesday we'll know." ◆

CHAPTER 6

OVERCOMING THE 'GHOSTS'

Finding redemption in the postseason

Snow sets the tone early in series opener against Atlanta

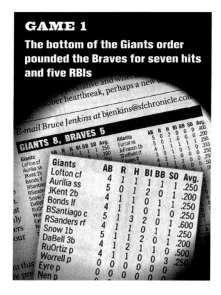

GAME 1

The bottom of the Giants order pounded the Braves for seven hits and five RBIs

OCT. 3, 2002

They savage him on the talk shows as if he hadn't done a decent thing in his life. Fans mutter and grumble in the stands of Pacific Bell Park, while journalists scoff heartlessly at his misfortune.

This has been one lousy year for J.T. Snow. How fitting it was, then, that Snow struck the first big blow of the Giants' postseason Wednesday, a two-run double in the second inning of their 8-5 win.

The pure athlete in him was revived, his reputation as a clutch player restored for at least one day.

It wasn't so long ago that Snow hit one of the most epic home runs in Giants history, the three-run, ninth-inning shot that tied Game 2 of the 2000 Division Series against the Mets. That was

BRUCE JENKINS

the Giants' last great October moment, as it turned out, and Snow's career didn't exactly take off, either. The past two seasons saw him hit .246, a noticeable regression that had critics calling for a new look at first base.

At this point, you wouldn't want to tinker with the Giants' lineup in any way. Every starter got at least one hit Wednesday in the type of classy, professional performance that had been anticipated by management all season.

None of the hits was quite as big as Snow's. Nobody needed one as badly, not even the October-weary Barry Bonds. When the team is winning and J.T. Snow is hitting, all seems right in the Giants' world.

The double came on an inside, 2-2 fastball from Tom Glavine. Snow hasn't been turning on the ball in the season's second half; Glavine figured he could

jam him, force a weak groundball or maybe even a strikeout.

Instead, Snow drilled it down the first-base line and into the right-field corner, giving Giants starter Russ Ortiz a 2-0 lead.

"Everybody in this clubhouse knows that J.T.'s gonna be there," said teammate Rich Aurilia. "He went through a rough stretch, but nobody has to tell us what kind of player he is. He's out there for a reason. For him to get a big hit off a tough lefty — that was huge."

Wearing the remnants of afternoon battle — the eye black reminiscent of a football player (or Will Clark) — Snow stood at his locker and spoke of patience, not revenge.

"I don't listen to that stuff on the radio," he said. "People have the right to call up and say what they want. I just go out and give everything I have to the team. I figure if you stay positive, all that other stuff takes care of itself."

The more tolerant observers have never wavered on Snow's status in the game. It was evident many miles away, at Yankee Stadium, in Game 1 of the Division Series against the Angels on Tuesday night. Jason Giambi hit a sharp but playable two-out grounder to Scott Spiezio, playing first base for the Angels, and Spiezio had it trickle off his glove into

the outfield for a run-scoring single, setting up Bernie Williams' stunning three-run homer. Snow makes that play in his sleep. Put him in the Bronx that night, and the Angels lead the series, 1-0.

Around the Bay Area, fans have been asking a bit more from him. On Wednesday, he delivered. October is a wonderful month for forgiveness. ◆

First baseman J.T. Snow, opposite page, silenced critics with a two-run double to ignite the offense in the first game against the Braves. Above, Jeff Kent completes a double play — one of three by the Giants that day — despite the efforts of Atlanta's Rafael Furcal to break up the play.

Settling for a split against the Braves

Atlanta reminds Giants who the wild-card team is with a pounding of Rueter

Giants shortstop Rich Aurilia flips the ball to Jeff Kent for a double play against the Braves in Game 2 of the National League Division Series.

OCT. 4, 2002

By Henry Schulman
CHRONICLE STAFF WRITER

ATLANTA — Barry Bonds' first postseason home run in 10 years was a screaming shot across the bow that did no damage. The crew aboard the Braves' ship was already partying from bow to stern, and Bonds was in no position to sink it.

The ninth-inning blast off closer John Smoltz was as meaningful as an episode of "Elimidate," a nice piece of eye candy in a 7-3 Atlanta victory Thursday night that evened the best-of-five National League Division Series at a win apiece.

After Game 1, the Giants sneered at talk of a split here. However, once the Braves stormed back to win Game 2, pounding Kirk Rueter, many in the visiting clubhouse treated the split as a grand success.

"I feel very good about the split," right fielder Reggie Sanders said. "Everybody has their work cut out for them now and it's not going to be an easy task. The postseason is all about fighting. Hopefully we'll bring it home."

If that was the right thing to say, per-haps first baseman J.T. Snow summarized the deeper feelings inside the club-house after the Giants' first defeat in two weeks.

"We wanted to win two," Snow said. "We didn't want to sell ourselves short. Why settle for five hundred when you can be a thousand?"

The Giants did fly home in position to capture the series without having to return to Turner Field if they win Games 3 and 4 at Pacific Bell Park this week-end. On the other hand, the Braves feel they wrested the series back to their camp, with playoff-seasoned Greg Mad-dux pitching the important swing game Saturday against October neophyte Ja-son Schmidt.

"Today was big," Smoltz said. "Their lineup was hot. This was the first time they lost in 10 games. It was the first time they fell behind in 80-some-thing innings. Our crowd was great and we established ourselves early. It was nice to win a must-win game."

For the second time in his career, Braves starter Kevin Millwood followed a Braves loss in the opener of a Division Series with a dominating Game 2 per-formance. In 1999, he one-hit the Hous-ton Astros. The Giants had a bit more success, getting solo homers from Snow and Rich Aurilia in Millwood's six in nings, far too little to match the damag against Rueter.

Javy Lopez, Vinny Castilla and Mar DeRosa, the 6-7-8 hitters, scored si runs and went 5-for-5 with a walk, sin gle, double, triple and two homers ove two turns against Rueter.

"It appeared they had a very goo game plan against Kirk," manage Dusty Baker said. ◆

GAME 2

The Braves' seven runs came in three innings against Kirk Rueter

Two little pitches, one Giant defeat

S.F. faces elimination after Atlanta takes advantage of baffled bullpen

OCT. 6, 2002

Since it is mathematically impossible to give up more than five runs in two pitches, Manny Aybar's name will be inextricably welded into the superstructure of Giant postseason disasters. After all, a bases-loaded single and a three-run homer in the time it takes to get halfway to the bathroom and then say, "Damn!" is a rarity at any level.

Then again, maybe Aybar can be an asterisk on an afterthought when the bigger picture is revealed. It all depends right now on what the Giants plan to do about Saturday's preposterous 10-1 loss to the Atlanta Braves in Game 3 of the NL Division Series.

"It doesn't matter how it happened," manager Dusty Baker said, fibbing only the slightest bit. "It only matters that

RAY RATTO

you lost, and whether you overcome it the next day."

Therein lies the local nine, yet again, backs against the band saw and needing Livan Hernandez to be as October as he can be.

Whether he can is an issue for this evening, and you can throw in all the offseason baggage you like. This is one of those moments that have confronted and defeated the Giants throughout their time in San Francisco, and Hernandez is being asked merely to reverse his regular season blahs and the tide of history.

For now, we know only how they got to this latest desperate strait, and though you may be desperate to blame Aybar for hanging a sinker to the deeply improbable Keith Lockhart, or Baker for not bringing in Trevor Hoffman, the truth lies elsewhere.

In the locker of Jason David Schmidt.

It was he, the Giants starting pitcher in this show-or-blow game, who suddenly turned unexpectedly wild and exasperatingly careful in the sixth inning, walking Gary Sheffield, Chipper Jones and Andruw Jones on 17 pitches and presenting Baker with a choice that he should not have been asked to make.

But more on that momentarily. I mean, you're sitting at your kitchen table in your robe and trying not to spill coffee on your stomach. You've got nowhere to go. Relax. We'll get there.

"I was probably a little bit careful," Schmidt said. "I maybe could have gone after Andruw a little bit more."

"It wasn't just two pitches that changed the game," Baker concurred. "It was more like 15."

Schmidt had gone head-to-head for five innings with Greg Maddux, the still-reigning maestro of the outside, and af-

Jeff Kent hangs his head after the Atlanta Braves score four runs in the ninth inning of Game 3.

ter a wasteful beginning had found his pace and retired 10 consecutive Braves. This game had all the marks of that rarity in this postseason — a pitchers' duel.

But it ended when Schmidt tried to out-Maddux Maddux, working away from the heart of the Atlanta order and leaving Aybar to tidy the mess.

So Aybar it was, and he threw a nasty little slider that broke Castilla's bat before sailing into left field to score Sheffield and Chipper Jones. Aybar followed that with an egregious error, a sinker inside that didn't sink or get inside that Lockhart turned into his 42nd career homer. Game over, although the rest of the Giant bullpen chipped in with a four-spot in the ninth to give that extra whiff of eggs gone bad to an already unhappy day for the locals. ◆

Livan large in crucial Game 4

Starter Hernandez at top of his game when calendar hits October

OCT. 7, 2002

He jogged in left field all by himself, warming up before the game, and the fans cheered as if they'd recovered a prodigal son. In a way, they had.

He stepped from the dugout in the top of the ninth, and they cheered again, more madly this time. They booed when Dusty Baker came out to the mound to remove him with one out.

The fans at Pacific Bell Park paid lavish tribute to Livan Hernandez Sunday night, roughly two months after they gladly would have paid for plane fare to send the pitcher anywhere else in the major leagues.

This is how a legend is reborn. The calendar turns to October, and Her-

GWEN KNAPP

nandez's right arm, leaden for so much of the season, turns to gold again.

He gave San Francisco another day in the National League playoffs with a masterful performance in Game 4 of the Division Series, beating the Braves 8-3. The Giants will go to Atlanta tonight for the deciding Game 5. Hernandez will go into the record books, in a tie with Hall of Famer Lefty Gomez for the most wins in the postseason (6) without a defeat.

Gomez finished up in 1938, which seemed to be about the last time Giants fans felt that they could count on Hernandez. He won a playoff game for them as recently as 2000, to go along with the four he won for Florida in 1997, but the last two years have been exasperating.

On any night, the Giants didn't know which Livan they would get. Would it be the Livan who could do it all — field beautifully, hit like an outfielder, and above all, pitch beguiling ball, throwing from so many different angles that batting against him is completely disorienting? Or would it be the Livan whose mind always seemed to be taking off in different angles?

In the postseason, there is no doubt. There is only one Livan — the money pitcher. With all due deference to Reggie Jackson, he is Senor Octubre.

Hernandez re-established that Sunday night, holding onto a no-hitter through four innings. When the Braves finally started hitting him, he pitched and fielded his way into a double play. He grabbed a throw from shortstop Rich Aurilia while running to first base and quickly stabbed his foot at the bag, beating Darren Bragg by a tiny fraction of a step.

J.T. Snow, no stranger to smooth fielding, said: "He made that play look a lot easier than it really is. . . . It's like anything when people are good at something. They make it look effortless."

His teammates don't exactly marvel at Hernandez's success in the postseason. They know him. They know what to expect.

"He has taken his lumps from people this year," Snow said, "but when we needed him the most, he was there. . . . You know he's not going to get rattled, he's going to have fun out there. I think players who are relaxed and know how to enjoy the playoffs do the best."

It's tempting to wonder how good he would be if he pitched all season as if it were October, or even at 80 percent of that intensity. Hernandez wouldn't be just a money pitcher then. He'd be rich enough to hire Kevin Brown as his chauffeur.

For most of 2002, he simply drove Giants fans crazy and almost, if he had been better trade bait, drove himself out of town. His 16 losses tied for the National League lead, which explains why his perfect record in the playoffs wasn't given the weight it deserved.

Jeff Brantley, doing ESPN commentary earlier in the day, dismissed it quickly. As soon as someone mentioned Hernandez's 5-0 mark, he said: "It will be 5-1 after tonight."

Hernandez heard about that comment and in the interview room after the game, he almost duplicated Brantley's snideness. "I'm 6-0 right now," he said, starting to shrug. "I'm sorry."

He had every right to be pleased. He had done everything a pitcher could do, avoiding trouble most of the night, brilliantly extricating himself from the occasional mess, and putting down two pretty sacrifice bunts.

Little Darren Baker follows his dad out of the Giants dugout, above, after their victory in Game of the division series against Atlanta. Far left, Livan Hernandez waves his hat at the crowd but he is not happy after being replaced just two outs shy of a complete game.

The first bunt earned him a mini-standing ovation in the second inning, before Hernandez had definitively proved that he was on top of things. The fans seemed to sense that, as a big-game pitcher, Hernandez would benefit from every little reminder that this was, in fact, a huge game. They praised him lavishly. In the end, so did the Braves.

Bobby Cox, their manager, still has complaints about the 1997 playoff game in which Hernandez benefited from a strike zone the size of a Winnebago. This time, the zone was fashion-model thin.

"I can guarantee you, he did not get one break all night," Cox said. "He pitched great."

The umpires had changed, but the notoriously inconsistent Hernandez remained the same. It was October, and he was unbeatable. ◆

GOING THE DISTANCE

Livan Hernandez came within two outs of being the first Giants pitcher in 15 years to toss a complete game in the postseason.

The six complete game pitchers in S.F. history:

■ **Mike Krukow** — 1987 LCS, Game 4 vs. Cardinals at Candlestick Park (4-2 victory)
■ **Dave Dravecky** — 1987 LCS, Game 2 vs. Cardinals at Busch Stadium (5-0 victory)
■ **Juan Marichal** — 1971 LCS, Game 3 vs. Pirates at Three Rivers Stadium (2-1 loss)
■ **Gaylord Perry** — 1971 LCS, Game 1 vs. Pirates at Candlestick Park (5-4 victory)
■ **Billy Pierce** — 1962 World Series, Game 6 vs. Yankees at Candlestick Park (5-2 victory)
■ **Jack Sanford** — 1962 World Series, Game 2 vs. Yankees at Candlestick Park (2-0 victory)

GAME 4

Live bats and clutch pitching against Braves keep Giants' playoff hopes alive

Bring on the Cards

Giants slay the 'beast of the East' Atlanta for title as Nen slams door in the 9th

OCT. 8, 2002

By Henry Schulman
CHRONICLE STAFF WRITER

ATLANTA — The carpet in the visiting clubhouse at Turner Field wears the stains of many champagne celebrations by teams that, in their own ways, played out unique stories and beat the Atlanta Braves in the postseason.

The Giants have poured another layer of bubbly on the rug, adding another chapter to their season-long tale of fortitude and perhaps allowing revisionists to rewrite the sad tome about Barry Bonds in the postseason.

With Bonds singling and scoring on a Reggie Sanders single, then hitting the most important home run of his career, the Giants beat the Braves 3-1 in the decisive fifth game of their National League Division Series Monday night. It was the first time in franchise history they won a winner-take-all game in the postseason.

"We'd stormed the castle a couple of times, but we'd never slain the dragon," general manager Brian Sabean said in a clubhouse celebration more raucous than most. "We got the beast of the East. We all know the pennant goes through Atlanta, and we beat them at their own game, pitching, which is to our credit."

Catcher Benito Santiago predicted the Giants would topple the Braves and couldn't wait to expand his psychic-hotline business.

"Now we're going to go all the way. Put it in the paper," Santiago said.

Closer Robb Nen overcame a frightful ninth inning and rewrote some history himself to earn the save, and the Giants became the first NL team to erase a deficit of two-games-to-one and win a Division Series since it was instituted in 1995.

Dusty Baker got his first playoff-series win in three tries as Giants manager, leading the team to its first NLCS since 1989 and bolstering the chances he will return next season. The Giants open the best-of-seven NLCS Wednesday night in St. Louis, with Kirk Rueter likely facing Matt Morris.

Bonds finally beat his rap as a postseason failure with his two key hits off Game 2 winner Kevin Millwood, including a 417-foot home run on a 3-2 fastball leading off the fourth inning. His opposite-field drive sliced through the cool October air and carried well into the bleachers.

Having come into the series with one postseason homer, off Atlanta's Tom Glavine in the 1992 NLCS, Bonds hit three in this series and nearly had five. Andruw Jones stole one with a leaping catch in Game 1, and Bonds sent Chipper Jones crashing into the left-field fence with a drive in Game 4.

Bonds, as usual, wanted to talk about the team's first postseason series victor during his 10 seasons as a Giant.

"It's just unfortunate that so muc emphasis is put on me as an individu than us as a team," he said.

His teammates were thrilled wit Bonds' performance: 5-for-17 wit three homers, four walks and four RBI

"If there's two guys I'm happiest fo Dusty is one and Barry is the other, shortstop Rich Aurilia said. "The gu gets such a bad rap for not producing i the postseason. He hit a huge home ru tonight. I hope that squelches all the tal of him not being a postseason player."

Russ Ortiz pitched 5⅓ innings of one run ball and became the first Giant t win twice in the same postseason serie since Carl Hubbell in the 1933 Worl Series.

Felix Rodriguez got two big outs, Kenny Lofton hit a sacrifice fly in the seventh for insurance and Tim Worrell overcame two horrible outings earlier in the series to protect the 3-1 lead in the seventh and eighth for Nen, whose worst moment of 2002 came on the Turner Field mound. On Aug. 15, Nen blew a 3-1 lead in the ninth by allowing a two-strike, two-out single to Chipper Jones. The game eventually was suspended by rain, tied 3-3.

Remarkably, Nen inherited the same 3-1 lead and had to face the same part of the Braves' order Monday night. Naturally, the Braves put two runners on with nobody out on a Jeff Kent throwing error and a Julio Franco single.

With runners on the corners, nobody out and 45,203 fans on their feet doing

their chop, Nen struck out Gary Sheffield on four pitches. Up stepped Jones, who ached to repeat history as much as Nen ached to prevent it.

Nen won. After throwing a fastball for a called strike, he threw a slider that Jones grounded to J.T. Snow, who stepped on first base for one out and then chased Franco toward second. Snow threw to Aurilia, who tagged Franco to complete the series-ending double play.

Nen said his August failure never entered his mind. "Back then, I was not quite as locked in as I am now," he said before dedicating his save to the fans back home. "This is for them, as much as they rallied behind me all year and put up with all my struggles,' he said. "They're the greatest fans in the world." ◆

GAME 5

Barry Bonds contributed two hits, including a solo homer in the fourth inning

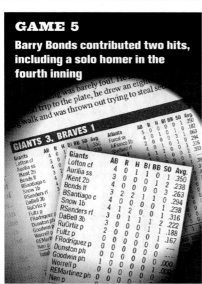

Defiant Lofton leads the charge

Bad blood starts to boil as Giants come out swinging against Cardinals

OCT. 10, 2002

ST. LOUIS — The Giants' first move was to grab the man himself. All hell was breaking loose at Busch Stadium, and they had to save Kenny Lofton from his instincts.

Lofton wanted a piece of pitcher Mike Crudale or anyone else throwing words his way. A "message" pitch had come down, pretty close to his head, and an all-out brawl was one punch from reality.

Benito Santiago got to Lofton, quickly, then Rich Aurilia and Tsuyoshi Shinjo, of all people. At that point, the Pac Bell ushers and mayor Willie Brown probably wanted to be there, too, for Lofton is no longer some nice midseason pickup for the Giants. He's got the keys to the engine.

Lofton was positively relentless Wednesday night, in the grand leadoff tradition of Lou Brock, Bobby Bonds and Rickey Henderson. He singled, he stole, he homered, he pestered. Over

BRUCE JENKINS

time you come to realize something about truly great athletes: Never, ever doubt them. At the age of 35, Kenny Lofton has an October stage in front of him, and you'd swear he was 10 years younger.

Lofton was a steady, invaluable contributor during the Atlanta series, but in Game 1 at Busch Stadium, he simply took over. He walked to open the game, soon to score on Benito Santiago's infield single. He got the two-out single that led to the four-run second, stealing second with a fabulous jump and brazenly steaming toward third as Rich Aurilia punched an RBI single to right. Then he pulled out the thunder, unleashing a solo homer to right field for 6-1 in the third.

Lofton got a huge kick out of that. This is one of his hidden specialties — at a shade under 6 feet and 175 pounds, he has hit five postseason home runs over the years — and he stopped for a few moments to watch the ball's flight. If you're a tradition-minded manager like the Cardinals' Tony La Russa, this amounts to a federal crime.

Truth be told, Lofton's flash of satisfaction was harmless and well deserved. But not for La Russa, one of the game's major hotheads when the blood starts boiling. He wanted some payback, and in the fifth inning, Crudale's first pitch to Lofton was dangerously inside at around shoulder height.

La Russa thought Lofton overreacted. So did a lot of people around Busch Stadium, even a few who follow the Giants. Perhaps both men got a little too hot, but at least they stayed in character. When Dusty Baker said "We don't start nothin', but we don't take nothin'," he was telling Lofton's

GAME 1

Kenny Lofton sparked the offense and Benito Santiago drove in four runs in the Giants win

Henry Schulman at hschul-
...@sfchronicle.com.

GIANTS 9, CARDINALS 6

Giants	AB	R	H	BI	BB	SO	Avg.
Lofton cf	4	3	2	1	1	0	.500
Aurilia ss	4	1	1	2	0	1	.250
JKent 2b	4	5	1	2	0	3	.400
Bonds lf	2	2	1	3	0	0	.500
BSantiago c	5	1	0	1	0	2	.600
Snow 1b	4	0	1	0	0	2	.250
RSanders rf	4	0	0	1	0	1	.000
DaBell 3b	3	0	0	0	1	1	.250
Rueter p	0	0	0	0	0	1	.000
FRodriguez p	0	0	0	0	0	0	.000
Worrell p	0	0	0	0	0	0	
Nen p	0	0	0	0	0	0	
Totals	36	9	11	9	5	7	

life story.

He's always been a very old soul, going back to his poverty-ridden youth East Chicago, Ind., and he has found many kindred spirits on a Giants team fielding an entire lineup of over-30 players. The hilarious, off-field banter between Lofton and backup outfielder Shawon Dunston has been especially rich, revealing a side of Lofton seldom seen in his career.

"He can be cold, and he can be frigid," one of his fraternity brothers at the University of Arizona once said. "It tough to know that person inside."

Defiant? He's got a right to be. Lofton's mother, Annie, was just 1... years old at the time of his birth. He never knew his dad, who passed in and out of Annie's life within weeks. Feeling ill-equipped to handle an infant son, Annie left East Chicago and moved to Alabama, leaving Kenny in the hands his grandmother, Rosie Person, a magnificently strong woman who, after losing her husband to bronchial pneumo...

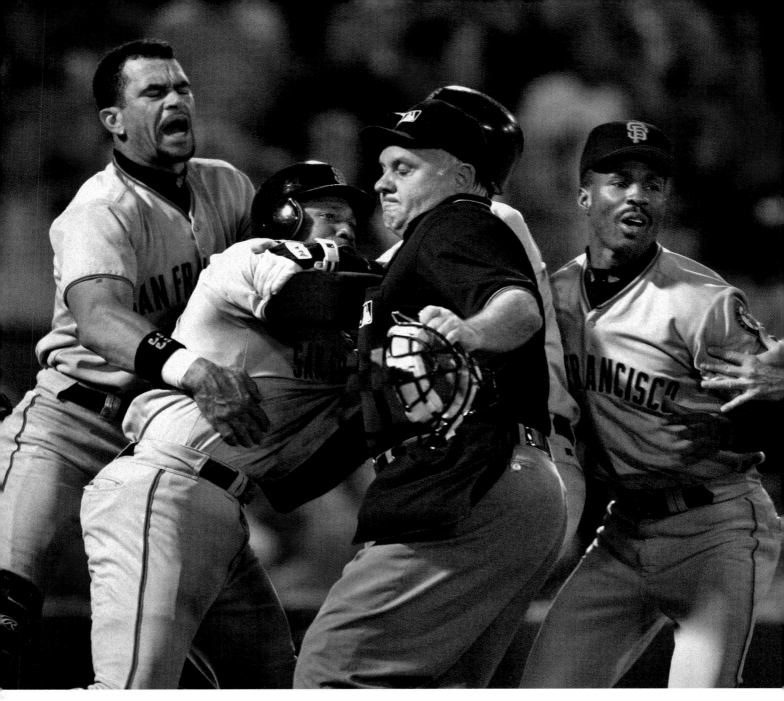

ia, raised her own seven children on lit-
le more than Social Security.

"Kenny was just a little tiny baby,
o more'n about 2½ pounds," Person
aid in a rare interview with the Day-
on Daily News in 1995. "His momma
vas scared to death to hold him, 'cause
he was afraid she'd drop him. So I
nade a little pillow and we carried him
round on that. One day Annie said, 'I
vant you to keep Kenny Man.' I
hought she was joking, but she said,
No, he's yours.'"

Little Kenny grew up strong, fearless.
riends said they never saw him cry. He
tayed in pleasant touch with his
nother, but his soft spot was for Rosie,
vho was going blind from glaucoma.

They lived in a friend's basement for a
while, then moved to a two-room apart-
ment where the windows were cracked,
the walls were bare and all the chair
backs were missing.

The years of hardship formed an often unapproachable wall around
Lofton, and nobody knew him quite like
Rosie. She became fond of the Chicago
Cubs' radio broadcasts, and with her
sight completely gone in the mid-'90s,
Kenny would come to visit, filling in the
information left unsaid. In the middle of
the seventh inning, Rosie would rise to
her feet. If there was no one else in the
room, Kenny would stand up with her.
And if no one else could hear, he would
sing "Take Me Out to the Ballgame"

with her.

That's the Giants' leadoff man, for
real. His interview-room expression
never changed after Wednesday night's
game, whether he was calling the playoffs "fun" or admitting, "We were kick-
ing their butts at the time."

But then someone told the ancient
Santiago, sitting next to Lofton at the
podium, that he'd played like a 20-year-
old out there. "Let me tell you something," Santiago said. "You said 20. I'm
26."

And Lofton suddenly smiled — a
handsome and winning smile. Very
slowly, the Giants are getting to know
their leadoff man. They're liking him
more every day. ◆

Home plate umpire Randy Marsh and catcher Benito Santiago (left) hold back Kenny Lofton, above, who was irate over Mike Crudale's brushback pitch in the fifth inning. Opposite page, Dusty Baker jokes with Cardinals players during pregame introductions.

Smell of success

Giants won't say it, but it looks like this one's in the bank

OCT. 11, 2002

ST. LOUIS — The St. Louis Cardinals are not so deficient a team that they cannot return to the Giants what the Giants have dumped on them these past two days.

But as a wise man with his kid's college fund sitting on Secretariat minus-29 lengths at the Belmont once said, that ain't the way to bet.

Indeed, anyone who heard the air sucked out of Busch Stadium when Jason Schmidt struck out Edgar Renteria to end the seventh inning of Thursday night's 4-1 victory surely believes that the Giants now have this series, and the Cardinals for that matter, by their re-

RAY RATTO

spective windpipes.

"Nobody here is taking anything for granted, believe me," general manager Brian Sabean said between phone calls from some of his new best friends. "Those guys are too good, and they've been through too much. But I'll tell you this. Our guys smell it now. They can smell it."

It's hard to know what mere smell gets you in baseball. You didn't see in any series preview the phrase, "NOSE: Edge, Giants."

I think that's one of those intangibles TV people use when their researchers haven't given them enough to say. But leaving this town two games to the good, given the Giants' postseason and Missouri-related histories . . . they'd be al-

lowed to talk a bit more than they have allowed themselves.

"This is baseball, and nothing surprises me," center fielder Kenny Lofton said when asked what the future holds after such a shiny present. "Anything can happen. I've seen it."

They've all seen it, but what they saw and more important what they did Thursday has left few doubters outside that pocket of America whose closets are filled with red pullover sweaters.

Indeed, it was the nuances more than the final score that ended debate so quickly. Two Rich Aurilia homers, the first on the game's fourth pitch . . . Jason Schmidt at his very best (though you may ignore the Busch Stadium radar gun, for it estimated one of Schmidt's fastballs at Mach 2) . . . Lofton's 140-foot throw to beat J.D. Drew's death-or-glory attempt to tie the game in the third . . . Ramon Martinez's suicide squeeze in the ninth, which is as pure finger-in-your-eye-to-the-second-knuckle as it gets.

And now they go home to their little seaside joint, a place where visiting teams die slow and painless deaths, with their most reliable starter (Russ Ortiz) and their best postseason starter (Livan Hernandez) still unused.

I mean, to see the underside of this situation for the Giants you've got to be the sort of person who doesn't want Reese Witherspoon as your neighbor because she doesn't put her cans at the curb on pickup day.

And here we even allow for the sight of Peter Magowan grinding the enamel off his teeth as it becomes increasingly clear that he will be married to That Manager for at least another two years. And better yet, for even more money than the $2.65 million Magowan is paying him this year. Oh, well . . . 2004 will

Cardinal J.D. Drew looks back at Giants' catcher Benito Santiago, above, to see if he held onto the ball after an attempt to score in the third inning. Drew was tagged out. Left, starting pitcher Jason Schmidt was at his best against St. Louis

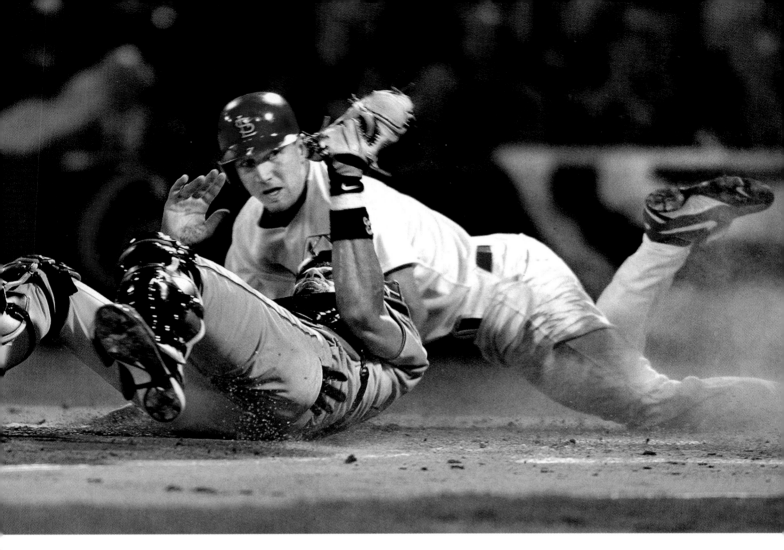

GAME 2

Jason Schmidt pitched seven scoreless innings and Rich Aurilia hit two home runs

be here before he knows it.

This is as good as it's ever gotten for the Giants in the postseason, two games to the good after two games. They led the Cardinals in '87, three games to two, but the first five games had been fire-fights and nobody expected anything different from 6 or 7. They pounded the Cubs easily in '89, but they were the better team and the Cubs were . . . well, the Cubs.

These Cardinals, though, entered the playoffs with a better pedigree, even without injured third baseman Scott Rolen. They were opening at home, in the galactic central point of the baseball universe. They were rested, their rotation was ordered for optimal results, and as Sabean said, they'd seen too much to be fazed by anything as modest as the first Giants' squeeze bunt in at least three years, by Baker's count.

"It was the perfect time because we had the perfect guy to do it," the manager said of Martinez. "He is one of the headiest guys we have. They (the Cardinals) even put a play on to see if he'd show bunt, and he didn't."

So now the circus heads west, with everything going San Francisco's way . . . which most longtime Giants fans know is the absolute worst time to be a Giants fan.

They will remind anyone who asks about the '85 Dodgers and Blue Jays, who won the first two games of their respective playoff series with the Cardinals and Royals at home but still crashed and burned. They'll even bring up the '82 Angels and '84 Cubs and '99 Indians and '01 A's, all of whom went up 2-0 in a five-game series and couldn't finish.

But that's out of 98 playoff series. The numbers don't support a lot of faith in the Cardinals.

Oh, you won't hear the Giants say it. Not yet, with two games still to win. The danger of premature hubris far exceeds any fear that Cardinals pitcher Chuck Finley can create in Game 3. Nothing's over until Bud Selig pushes a trophy into your chest and says, "Now try to be on time next Saturday, OK fellas?"

But to see a downside awaiting the Giants is to operate purely on lack of faith, on a pathological belief that anything that can happen will happen to, rather than for, the Giants. And so far in this series, nothing has happened to them that they haven't immediately turned into roses.

Maybe that's the smell Sabean was talking about Thursday night. ◆

One big hit not enough

Cardinals answer Bonds blast with one of their own to take Game 3

OCT. 13, 2002

By Henry Schulman
CHRONICLE STAFF WRITER

This National League Championship Series figured to be a great matchup because the Giants and Cardinals are both populated by seasoned, intelligent players who are blessed with the ability to work with blinders on and ignore the mayhem around them.

The Giants pulled it off in St. Louis, taking command of the series by playing two great games in a hostile environment.

The Cardinals may have overcome a stiffer challenge in Game 3 Saturday when they beat the Giants 5-4 and halved San Francisco's lead in the best-of-seven series to two games to one.

When Barry Bonds crushed a magnificent three-run homer into McCovey Cove in the fifth inning, tying a game the Giants trailed 4-1, a million volts of electricity shot through Pacific Bell Park.

The place buzzed louder than the Blue Angel jets that flew over the stadium. A crowd of 42,177 was certain the Giants would win.

The Cardinals weren't.

With the fans still murmuring over Bonds' blast against Chuck Finley, St. Louis left fielder Eli Marrero hit Jay Witasick's second pitch of the next inning into the left-field bleachers to restore the Cardinals' lead. Their bullpen did the rest, and the Giants were left to lick their wounds after stranding the bases loaded three times.

Reggie Sanders, 0-for-13 in the series and 4-for-31 this postseason, left eight men on base himself.

Catcher Mike Matheny, who hit one of three Cardinals homers in the first NLCS game at Pac Bell, was impressed with the way his team overcame Bonds' dramatic home run.

"There's no mapped-out book for it. You just adjust," Matheny said. "The situation was definitely deflating when we lost the lead. When you lose a three-run lead on one swing, it's definitely a

turn of the tide. It was nice the way El came out and quickly got it back for us."

Had the Giants won, Bonds' home run would have stood as one of the most important moments in franchise history. After Rich Aurilia walked and Jeff Kent singled to open the fifth, Bonds turned on a fastball boring in on his hands and somehow managed to hit it high, straight and very far into the bay, where a kayaker retrieved it.

"He really crushed that one," said catcher Benito Santiago, who was on deck for all four of Bonds' homers this postseason. "Typical Barry. He hit that one probably 600 feet."

The homer became a memorable footnote to a game in which the Giants gave away the first two St. Louis runs and failed to make hay of all the opportunities they had. The Cardinals practically begged the Giants to blow them out with some shoddy and bizarre defense in the first two innings, but it never happened.

It was a shock to see the Giants leave so many runners on base after they scored

Cardinal fan Todd Schrewe sneaks a peak at Game 3 of the series on a TV in the limo that is about to take him and his new wife, Kristin, to their wedding reception. They just had some of their wedding photos taken near Stan Musial's statue outside Busch Stadium.

Barry Bonds watches a three-run blast head for McCovey Cove during the fifth inning, left. The home run tied the game at 4-4. Below, Kannon Kile, son of the Cardinal pitcher Darryl Kile, takes the field with the Cardinals during team introductions.

3 of their 37 runs over the first seven games of the postseason with two out.

"Things are going to happen," Aurilia said. "You can't expect us to go out every day and get six hits in a row and two-out RBIs all the time. It's not going to happen. When you come through so many times in the first seven games and you don't come through in one game, it's kind of magnified."

The Giants loaded the bases in the first inning thanks in part to an error by shortstop Edgar Renteria and his throw to second baseman Fernando Vina on an attempted force at second. Inexplicably, Vina was 10 feet from the bag at the time. But Sanders flied out to strand all three.

The Giants loaded them again with nobody out in the second on singles by J.T. Snow and David Bell and a Russ Ortiz bunt that nobody could field, but all

they got was an Aurilia sacrifice fly. Kent singled to reload the bases, but Bonds flied out.

Down 5-4 in the seventh, the Giants got a leadoff double from Aurilia but never got Kent home. Dave Veres struck out Kent, walked Bonds intentionally and, after a Santiago infield hit loaded the bases, struck out Sanders. Steve Kline relieved Veres and retired Snow on a groundball.

Closer Jason Isringhausen walked Bonds with one out in the ninth but retired the last two Giants, Santiago and Sanders, for his third save of the post-season.

Manager Dusty Baker has said he might start Tom Goodwin over the struggling Sanders in Game 5 against Matt Morris because Sanders has never had a hit off the Cardinals' ace. But

Baker said Sanders would start Game 4 tonight against Andy Benes.

"He's a streaky hitter," Baker said, "and Reggie is one of the reasons we're here, know what I mean?" ◆

Benito Bambino!

Santiago uncorks a blast that puts San Francisco one win away from Series

OCT. 14, 2002

Baseball might be a kid's game, but right now, nobody is playing that game better than the old-timers known as the Giants.

Sunday night, the hero was the Giant who looks like he's 50 and was washed up three years ago.

Here's your Defining Moment of the season so far, Giants fans. Full count to Benito Santiago, bottom of the eighth inning at Pacific Bell Park, 2-2 tie with the Cardinals, two out, Barry Bonds on first, the Giants struggling on offense with three lousy hits on the night.

The Giants are being badly out-hit by the Cards, and looking like a team about to see its 2-1 series lead become null and void right in its own little ballpark on a cool, gray San Francisco night, heartbreak weather.

Boom, Santiago launches a mile-high howitzer shot deep into the left-field bleachers. And because that wasn't

SCOTT OSTLER

enough drama, Giants' closer Robb Nen gives up a run in the ninth and has two runners on base with two out when he strikes out J.D. Drew on a 3-2 fastball.

Sunday night's amazing win goes to Santiago, a gentleman in essentially his second career, creases on his face deeper than a Russian novel, legs aching from seven months of squatting behind the plate, but in a fine hitting groove.

Every time the enemy team works around Bonds, as they do almost every at-bat these days, here comes Santiago, raisin' hell. He hit .278 in the regular season, with power, when the Giants would have been thrilled with .240. In the postseason, he's got 11 RBIs, and in four games against the Cards, he's got six hits, two homers.

He strides to the plate with a look that's almost smug, as if to say, "Go ahead and walk Barry. I understand. I'll just get up here and take my hacks."

And time after time, Benny makes 'em pay.

It makes you realize you should never even try to figure out this game. Santiago has no business wreaking this kind of havoc at age 37, long after his career went into decline due to too much partying, an auto accident and old age.

With age comes wisdom, ideally.

"What I remember (when batting in the eighth inning)," Santiago said, "was that he (reliever Rick White) struck me out on the same pitch (in the sixth)."

In other words, Santiago figures they'll try to get him again with the same fastball in. Santiago is a catcher, he goes up to bat thinking, working the chess board in his head.

Santiago said afterward that he remembers being rescued from baseball's scrap heap two springs ago.

"Dusty give me that phone call," Santiago said, referring to manager Dusty Baker. "He really signed me up. I couldn't wait to go to San Francisco and play for this man."

That's a classic Dusty story. Players love to play for him. And remember, this is the manager who might be gone when the Giants' October run is over, due to a combination of his dissatisfaction with management, and theirs with him. If that rift can be healed, Sunday night's game was a starting point.

Sunday's heroes were all Dusty Guys, players the skipper has shown great faith in despite evidence to the contrary, guys he sticks with in the face of varying degrees of criticism and second-guessing.

Such as J.T. Snow. The Giants were down 2-0 going into the bottom of the sixth last night, two out, and Snow rocketed a two-run double to center. Snow kept his first base job this season mainly

Barry Bonds, above, exults as he rounds the bases after Benito Santiago's eighth-inning two-run homer, which broke a 2-2 tie. Cardinals manager Tony La Russa had opted to walk Bonds and face Santigo, right, who gets a warm welcome at home from J.T. Snow and Bonds.

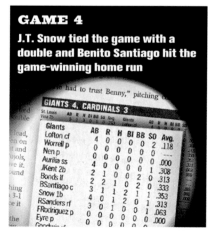

GAME 4
J.T. Snow tied the game with a double and Benito Santiago hit the game-winning home run

...had to trust Benny," pitching

GIANTS 4, CARDINALS 3

St. Louis	AB	R	H	BI	BB	SO	Avg.
Vina 2b							.263

Giants	AB	R	H	BI	BB	SO	Avg.
Lofton cf	4	0	0	0	0	2	.118
Worrell p	0	0	0	0	0	0	---
Nen p	0	0	0	0	0	0	---
Aurilia ss	4	0	0	0	0	0	.000
JKent 2b	4	0	0	0	0	1	.308
Bonds lf	2	1	0	0	2	0	.313
BSantiago c	3	1	1	2	0	0	.333
Snow 1b	3	1	1	2	1	1	.353
RSanders rf	3	0	1	0	0	1	.313
FRodriguez p	0	0	0	0	0	0	.063
Eyre p	0	0	0	0	0	0	.000

because there was nobody else, and because he's still an acrobat at the bag, but killed a million rallies with his anemic bat. In the playoffs, he has rediscovered his stroke.

And how about Livan Hernandez, the Giants' starting pitcher, who lost 16 games this year and seemed to lead the league in meatballs served up — and consumed? Sunday he gave up two runs to the first six Cardinal batters, then slammed the door for the next seven innings.

Suddenly the Giants, who had to battle to get into the postseason tournament, are looking like a team of destiny.

A very old team of destiny.

And with all due credit to Santiago, Snow and the other ancient Giants, the whole show still revolves around the sizzling senior citizen, Bonds. He has created an unsolvable problem like nothing before in baseball history.

In that eighth inning, Bonds came to bat with two outs, nobody on. The book says you never intentionally put the potential go-ahead run on base, but there's a new book, all about Barry.

Cards' manager Tony La Russa didn't even hesitate, ordering Bonds to be intentionally walked. La Russa's a macho guy who loves to come right at you, but he's no fool.

Bonds had already singled sharply and grounded out sharply. He's been hitting everything on the nose for two amazing years.

Every time Bonds steps to the plate now, it's "Casey at the Bat" on the drama scale. All the talk about Barry's failures in postseasons past is now ancient news. Now the talk is that you pitch to this guy at your peril, and whenever possible, you walk him and take the bat out of his hands. And you take your chances with the old man, Santiago. ◆

Finally clinched

Lofton laughs last as Giants take NL pennant

OCT. 15, 2002

By Henry Schulman
CHRONICLE STAFF WRITER

Dusty Baker stood with his team on the steps of the dugout and the precipice of history when his 3-year-old son Darren turned to him and explained the situation, just in case it wasn't clear.

"Daddy," he said, "one more hit from Kenny Lofton and we win the game."

On cue, Lofton swung at the only pitch the unfortunate Steve Kline would throw and delivered the Giants to their third World Series since they moved to San Francisco in 1958.

His two-out single to right in the ninth, following singles by David Bell and talk-show scourge Shawon Dunston, beat the Cardinals 2-1 at Pacific Bell Park Monday night, giving San Francisco the National League Championship Series four games to one.

Bell is not the fastest man in the big leagues, but when Lofton's ball sailed into right field, he found wings. Bell bolted from second base, rounded third without a moment's hesitation and charged toward home plate.

Right fielder J.D. Drew heaved a mighty throw home, but it was wide right. Bell morphed into Pete Rose. Bell lunged into the air headfirst. When he landed on the dish, the Giants had the pennant and 42,673 fans at Pacific Bell Park had just cause to go berserk.

Ten years after Baker became manager and Barry Bonds came home, they finally danced together as league champions, with a chance to bring the Giants their first World Series championship since 1954.

Somebody asked Baker if he finally got the monkey off his back.

"There ain't no monkey on my back," he replied. "The monkey's in Anaheim."

The Giants will be there, too, starting Saturday, when they open the first all-wild-card World Series against the Angels at Edison Field.

Leave it to first baseman J.T. Snow to place this accomplishment in perspective. He was measured all season by what he failed to do instead of what he did do. The same could be said for the team.

"When you play this game long enough, you realize personal things don't mean as much," Snow said. "It's all about winning. People are going to remember championships. They're not going to know 10 or 15 years down the road what your batting average was or how many home runs you had.

"We played like champions against the Braves, and we played like champions against the Cardinals."

St. Louis might have scripted its own demise. Lofton had homered off Matt Morris in Game 1. He stopped to admire the flight of the ball, and next time up he was brushed back by a high-and-tight pitch. The benches cleared. After that incident, Lofton went 16 at-bats without a hit.

Then, in the fourth inning Monday night, Morris fired his first pitch into Lofton's back. The next time up, in the sixth, Lofton singled to break the hitless streak. He singled again in the eighth and later scored on Bonds' sacrifice fly, tying the game 1-1.

With two out in the ninth — didn't it have to start with two out? — Bell lined a single to left. Dunston, who would be in tears later in the clubhouse, approached the plate for the third time in the series.

Dunston came through, lofting a single to center that moved Bell to second and finally knocked out Morris after an

Tim Worrell sprays Tom Goodwin with champagne in the Giants clubhouse, above, after the team's victory in Game 5. Kenny Lofton celebrates his ninth inning game-winning single, top; fans Rick Swig, left, and Chip Conley celebrate the Giants victory, left.

xceptional start. In came the left-han-
er Kline. Up stepped Lofton, still sore
rom where Morris drilled him.

"Sometimes you have to let sleeping
ogs lie," Lofton said in what could be
he epitaph for the Cardinals' season.
They ended up hitting me, but I kept
my focus. I said, 'I'm going to get you
ooner or later.' "

It turned out to be later.

"It was a slider," Lofton said of the
ennant-clinching single. "Once it went
ver (Fernando) Vina's head, I was a
retty excited guy. I'm going, 'David,
ou've gotta score! You've gotta
core!' "

Bell took off from second and got the
o' sign from third-base coach Sonny
ackson. When he started his headfirst
ive, Bell had no idea the throw was off-
ine. As he landed on the plate, he saw
atcher Mike Matheny move right to get

the ball.

"It was a relief, a great feeling," Bell
said. "I looked up and I saw Richie (Aurilia), and it was the best feeling in the
world."

Then, bedlam.

Lofton was hoisted into the air.
Bonds flew out of the dugout as if he
were shot by a cannon. Livan Hernandez was dancing. Players piled into each
other in one joyous collision after another. The party started at second base,
moved into the clubhouse, then returned
to the field, where the players provided
a victory lap for the fans.

There, series MVP Benito Santiago
became a champagne magnet. The man
who keeps predicting wins for the Giants lapped it up.

"Oh my God, this is a dream come
true, and that's what you play for," Santiago said. "It's been a long time behind

the plate and taking foul tips. It's great,
but hey, it can be better. Now we just
have to go all the way." ◆

GAME 5

**Kenny Lofton scored a run and
drove in the winning run; Kirk
Rueter pitched six scoreless
innings**

hulman@sfchronicle.com.

Giants	AB	R	H	BI	BB	SO	Avg.
Lofton cf	4	1	3	1	0	0	.238
Aurilia ss	4	1	1	0	0	1	
JKent 2b	2	0	1	0	0	1	
Bonds lf	3	0	0	0	1	0	.333
BSantiago c	2	0	1	1	0		.263
Goodwin rf	3	0	0	1	1	0	.273

St. Louis	IP	H	R	ER	BB	SO	NP	ERA
Morris L (0-2)	8⅓	6	2	2	2	4	100	6.23
Kline	0	0	0	0	0	0	1	0.00

Giants	IP	H	R	ER	BB	SO	NP	ERA
Rueter	6	6	0	0	1	2	95	4.09
FRodriguez	1	2	1	1	0	0	22	1.93
Eyre	⅓	0	0	0	0	1	4	0.00
Worrell W (2-0)	1⅔	1	0	0	0	2	21	2.08

Kline pitched to 1 batter in the 9th.
IBB—off Morris (Bonds) 1. HBP—by Morris (JKent), by Morris (Aurilia), by Morris (Lofton).
Umpires—Home, Tim Welke; First, Charlie Reliford; Second, Randy Marsh; Third, Nelson; Left, Dale Scott; Right, Jeff Kellogg.
Time—3:01. Attendance—42,673 (41,467).

000 000 10

Dream fulfilled

Resurrection lifts Santiago from injury, career low to division series MVP

OCT. 19, 2002

*By Ron Kroichick
and Gwen Knapp*
CHRONICLE STAFF WRITERS

Benito Santiago wandered into the clubhouse in Scottsdale, Ariz., on March 20, 2001. He arrived as a fallen prodigy, a once-brash All-Star reduced to sitting at home, unwanted, until the Giants offered him a job late in spring training.

"Don't worry, guys," Santiago announced, in his clipped English, to his new teammates. "I'm not as old as I look." The players burst out laughing.

Yes, J.T. Snow recalled thinking, Santiago would fit in quite nicely.

Still, this exceeds even the wildest expectations: Tonight, the Giants meet the Anaheim Angels in Game 1 of the World Series. One major reason is Benito Rivera Santiago, the itinerant 37-year-old catcher with the weathered face, the one-time wonder-kid who returned from a car crash to resurrect his fading career.

Less than 19 months after his self-deprecating introduction, Santiago hit one of the biggest home runs in Giants history in Game 4 of the National League Championship Series. He was named Most Valuable Player of the series, helping the Giants win the pennant for the first time since 1989.

As champagne sprayed throughout the clubhouse Monday night, trainer Stan Conte found Santiago in the trainers' room — standing all alone, facing the wall, overcome by emotion.

"After everything I went through, I never thought this would happen in my whole life," Santiago said in the first-base dugout Thursday at Edison Field, after the Giants completed their first

World Series workout in Anaheim. "I dreamed it. I always dreamed it since I was a little kid."

The dream did not start to come true until Santiago lived through a nightmare. It started on Jan. 4, 1998, when he seemed to have the world at his disposal and abundant tomorrows to become a great player with a World Series ring.

He was at the wheel of his yellow 1997 Ferrari, a $135,000 toy, with his boat mechanic in the passenger seat. They were headed to a marina, zooming along a Florida street, many miles and several million dollars away from his impoverished upbringing in Puerto Rico.

Fort Lauderdale police estimated Santiago was driving 60 mph, in a 35 mph zone, when he hit a dip in the road, spun out of control and crashed into a tree. The mechanic, Francisco Arroyo, and Santiago survived, Arroyo with a broken leg and torn calf muscle and the catcher with a concussion, lacerations on his face, fractured vertebra in his back and ligament damage in his right knee.

Santiago played in only 15 games that season for Toronto, bothered by lingering knee pain. His body recovered, but his youth ended that day.

Santiago had a $4 million guaranteed salary with Toronto in 1998, but he has not approached that level of pay since the accident. The Giants signed him at a base salary of $500,000 last year; they paid him $2 million this season.

Yet when Santiago talks about the accident, he emphasizes what he gained from it — maturity, contentment and a new respect for the game of baseball.

Santa Isabel is a town of 20,000 people on the southern coast of Puerto Rico. That's where Santiago's grandparents raised him, essentially, after his father, Jose, died of cancer in 1965 when Benito was an infant. His athleticism and

powerful arm persuaded San Diego Padres officials to sign him as a teenager; he made his major-league debut in September 1986.

Talk to Santiago's former Padres teammates and a common theme emerges. They are happy he reached the World Series, pleased he is coaxing results out of that 37-year-old body — because he squandered some prime years.

Santiago often heard the refrain in his early days in the majors: He took his talent for granted. Study scouting reports? Not when your arm and bat are turbocharged, not when you are young, rich and brimming with self-confidence.

During his six years with San Diego, he won the 1987 National League Rookie of the Year award and set a rookie record with a 34-game hitting streak. He seemed like the game's next great catcher, Johnny Bench with flair.

But the flair sometimes became extreme off the field. It was not unusual for Santiago to climb into a limousine after games and find the nearest club. And then the next club. And so on, to the point where late nights blended into early mornings.

He was hardly a picture of restraint

Benito Santiago makes a curtain call to fans, right, after a grand slam against the Pittsburgh Pirates. The catcher jokes with teammates that he's not as old as he looks.

n the field, either. Tony Gwynn, a future Hall of Famer and Santiago's teammate in San Diego, recalled Santiago always trying to hit home runs, with little regard for the strike zone. "He swung at absolutely everything," Gwynn said. "No discipline whatsoever."

Santiago sparkled on defense, earning four consecutive All-Star berths, but even there he clashed with teammates. He frequently irritated his own pitching staff with his know-it-all manner.

Santiago has clearly evolved in the wake of his baseball odyssey; he made six stops after San Diego before finally landing with the Giants. He seldom swings at bad pitches anymore, and he does not always try to pull the ball toward left field.

So as he prepares for his debut in baseball's grand show, the question is natural: Does Santiago look back with some regret, knowing his career could have been better?

"Yes, that's a question in there," he said, "but I don't double-guess myself. That's why I wanted to change my mentality when I could still play. If you wait until you go home (for retirement), that's when you get sad.

"I want to finish my career so that I am proud of myself, not as a player who had a bad reputation." ◆

CHAPTER 8

CALIFORNIA SERIES

The Series has arrived

OCT. 22, 2002

By Henry Schulman
CHRONICLE STAFF WRITER

On a crisp October afternoon, standing inside a ballpark that he and his partners built with their own capital and credit, Giants owner Peter Magowan watched a 10-year-old dream unfold.

The players who take his checks were taking hacks in the batting cage at Pacific Bell Park, preparing for a night that many local curmudgeons figured they would never see.

The World Series returns to San Francisco tonight when the Giants host the Angels in Game 3.

The Series is tied at one win apiece, with the next three games set to light up China Basin, and Magowan is beside himself with joy. The controversies seem a million miles away.

"There's no way to describe it," he said. "It's a fantastic opportunity for our fans and our city. For someone who loves the game of baseball, this is the pinnacle of what we strive for. We've been going at it the last 10 years. We've come very close on a number of occasions.

"There's a tremendous sense of excitement, fulfillment and happiness for our fans, who stuck by us so loyally. There's a sense of elation, happiness, pride and anticipation."

In the Giants' clubhouse, there was also relief that they left the noise of Edison Field for their own noise at Pac Bell. "It's good to be home," outfielder Reggie Sanders said. ◆

Warming up: Jeff Kent and his son, Hunter, lead the team in practice, above; Barry Bonds, flanked by his two personal publicists, left, warms up for reporters' questions. Far right, Giants fan Janie Garcia, of San Francisco, shows her allegiance — and how she feels about the monkey — before Game 3 at Pacific Bell Park.

Worst seat better than best TV

OCT. 23, 2002

By Carl Nolte
CHRONICLE STAFF WRITER

Things were a bit grim Tuesday night out in the bleachers, out where the real fans hang out — not the celebrities, the visiting CEOs, the east coast guys in suits and wool topcoats — ordinary people.

At the World Series, though, even the cheap seats cost $60 a pop, and there is no such thing as a poor fan. But there are lucky ones who stood in line, or who got a ticket as a present, or who were given tickets, like a gift from the gods.

It was better than television, a thousand times better, they said, out in the hill in the bleachers in the World Series.

You had to be there, had to BE THERE.

"I think I'm the luckiest fan in baseball," said Anne Henline of Oakland, who got the ticket through the kindness of a friend. "Nobody wants to miss a second of this," she said. "The best teams in all of baseball to decide who gets the ring, who picks up all the marbles."

"I love the bleachers," said Erika Reyes of San Francisco, sitting in the next row down, section 138. "The box seats are more corporate, but out here, the official American sport is alive and well."

In the beginning, it was electric: Tony Bennett sang "America the Beautiful," holding on to the notes, an old pro, perfect for the gray evening. Oddly, no one sang the National Anthem.

That's rare, said Dominic Balsamo, a spokesman for Major League Baseball, but it has been done before. The last time

was the 2001 World Series.

But in the bleachers, no one noticed.

In the ballpark, in the bleachers especially, they gave the home team a standing ovation, and they shouted in delight again at the first pitch: a strike by Giants pitcher Livan Hernandez to the Angels David Eckstein. It was 5:30 p.m. and the World Series was on. ◆

DEANNE FITZMAURICE (TOP), CHRIS STEWART (RIGHT) / THE CHRONICLE

Bonds announces series with a bang

Giants set tone for game with the long ball — and another, and another

OCT. 20, 2002

By Henry Schulman
CHRONICLE STAFF WRITER

ANAHEIM — It took Barry Bonds 17 years to get into the batter's box at a World Series, and he was not about to stand there like a tree and let the moment pass him by.

Bonds turned on the fourth pitch he saw Saturday night and cranked it out of the park.

It felt good then and felt great a few hours later, for Bonds' fifth home run of this postseason led a 4-3 victory over Anaheim, the Giants' first triumph in a World Series game since 1962.

To heck with the Angels' nouveau-red fans and their infernal Rally Monkey, the Giants declared. For the third time this postseason, they invaded a hostile park and took the opening game.

Nobody was happier than Bonds, who lost his who-cares attitude about hitting home runs sometime during his second-inning trot as he became the oldest man ever to go deep in his first World

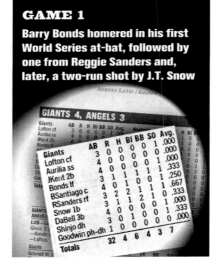

GAME 1

Barry Bonds homered in his first World Series at-bat, followed by one from Reggie Sanders and, later, a two-run shot by J.T. Snow

ADRESS LATIF / Reuters

GIANTS 4, ANGELS 3

Giants	AB	R	H	BI	BB	SO	Avg.
Lofton cf	3	0	0	0	0	1	.000
Aurilia ss	4	0	0	1	1	1	.333
JKent 2b	3	1	1	0	0	1	.250
Bonds lf	4	0	1	1	1	0	.667
BSantiago c	3	2	2	1	0	1	.333
RSanders rf	3	1	0	0	0	1	.000
Snow 1b	4	0	0	0	0	0	.333
DaBell 3b	3	0	0	0	0	0	.000
Shinjo dh	1	0	0	0	0	0	.000
Goodwin ph-dh	1	0	0	0	0	0	
Totals	**32**	**4**	**6**	**4**	**3**	**7**	

Series at-bat.

"Oh yeah, this is a dream come true. I finally made it to the game," he said, revealing the secret to his success this postseason. "I just feel right now we got through our ghosts of the past, the Braves, who've haunted me for years. That was a big key for me."

That sigh was nothing compared to the collective exhalation the Giants made when Robb Nen got Darin Erstad to fly out and end the first-ever Series game between two wild-card teams.

The Angels really should not rally around a monkey. Their persona is more like one of those little yip-yip dogs that will bite your ankles off if you can't shake them. In either of the Giants' first two playoff series, the 4-1 lead they built on second-inning homers by Bonds and Reggie Sanders, and native son J.T. Snow's two-run shot in the sixth, might have allowed them to rest easy.

Not here. Not against these Angels.

The Angels scored twice in the bottom of the sixth off Jason Schmidt, one on Troy Glaus' second homer, the other on a two-out RBI single by Adam Kennedy, to make it a one-run game.

The Giants needed their bullpen to be brilliant over the last 3½ innings, and it was. Felix Rodriguez, Tim Worrell and Nen ignored the noise, fended off the monkey and protected that slim lead without allowing a hit.

"There are mentally strong guys in this bullpen," said Schmidt, who won his second game of this postseason.

The Giants showed their collective mental acuity throughout the game in what easily was the loudest venue they've visited this October. There must be something to this monkey business, too, because the Angels scored their two sixth-inning runs right after he started going bananas on the videoboard.

"I didn't see the monkey grab a bat and get a hit," shortstop Rich Aurilia said in rebuttal. "I got a laugh in the ninth inning when they did that 'Risky Business' routine and the monkey slid across the floor instead of Tom Cruise."

The Giants had the last laugh — and the first one, too.

After Jarrod Washburn fell behind Bonds 2-0 leading off the second inning, Bonds swung and missed at a fastball. Washburn threw another one. Bonds didn't miss. He blasted it over the fence down the right-field line to give the Giants a 1-0 lead.

Washburn responded by grinning. "I had to smile," he said. "He's one of the greatest players in the game and he hit one off me. He's hit 600-some in his career, so I'm not the first. What else are you going to do? I made a mistake. He hit a home run. I had to chuckle and say 'Yeah, the guy is good.'"

One out later came a more shocking blow. Sanders, who was 1-for-16 in the NLCS against St. Louis, welcomed him

self to his second consecutive World Series by driving a home run the other way into the bleachers in right-center.

Snow's two-run homer to center in the sixth, following a two-out single by Sanders, was a great moment for the Orange County native. Just as critical was a defensive play he made. With the Giants leading 2-1, runners on the corners and one out in the fifth, No. 3 hitter Tim Salmon hit a high pop foul on the right side. Snow ran a long way from first base, got to the mesh screen, then slipped on a piece of tartan warning track, falling on his back. But he got up and made the catch for the second out. Schmidt then struck out Garret Anderson to leave the runners on base.

Snow was livid about the condition of the warning track. "I can't believe Major League Baseball didn't find that and do something with it," he said. "The last thing I expected was to run out there and slip on my back. That's not up to major-league standards in my mind."

Once again, the Giants struck first, on the road, which bodes well for them. On the other hand, the Angels lost the first two games of both AL playoff series and came back to beat the Yankees and Twins. Something has to give, but the Giants like their chances.

"We're playing good away," catcher Benito Santiago said. "That doesn't happen much in the regular season, but we did it in Atlanta, we did it in St. Louis and we did it against these guys. It's a good feeling." ◆

J.T. Snow shined on offense – a two-run homer in the sixth inning, left – and on defense, opposite page, with an acrobatic catch after stumbling. Above, Angels fan Jimmy Silva, 23, of Anaheim, makes his way to his seat during Game 1.

Power barrage lights up Edison

Angels on top when dust clears from 11-10 slugfest in Anaheim

OCT. 21, 2002

ANAHEIM — Remember way back when baseball was dull? When it was as boring as watching Rich Aurilia's goatee grow?

Like back near the end of August when the Giants were 11½ games out of first place and the games dragged on like bad blind dates?

Meet the New and Improved Baseball. Sunday night the Angels evened the World Series at 1-1 with an 11-10 win, in a brisk (or so it seemed) four hours (technically, 3:57).

Barry Bonds bombed a solo home run with two outs in the ninth, but Benito Santiago flied out.

Cumulative two-game score: Giants 14, Angels 14.

Game 1 was a tightly played thriller, but Sunday's whackfest at Edison Field, home of the Stepford Fans, had the wild/wooly feel of a rec-league softball game, although commissioner Bud Selig nixed the idea of a keg at second base.

The two teams knocked out 28 hits

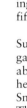

SCOTT OSTLER

Sunday and threw in some bungling and assorted excellent play, then packed up the whole crazy circus and rolled north for Games 3, 4 and 5 this week at Pac Bell Park.

The Angels scored five runs in the first inning, before the sun had set behind the grandstands, taking an insurmountable lead that the Giants surmounted by taking a 9-7 lead in the top of the fifth.

Six homers were struck Sunday, bringing the two-game total to 11. Theories abound. Steroids in the Anaheim drinking-water supply? Smog is thinner than real air? The World Series balls have a core of Flubber?

The homer barrage is unlikely to continue at Pac Bell Park, because the park is more spacious than Edison Field, and the Pac Bell air is heavy with fumes from garlic fries.

But some elements of the series are sure to continue. The Angels will be bringing their rally monkey north with them.

I'm referring, of course, to David Eckstein, the Angels' 5-foot-6 shortstop and leadoff man. Eckstein, rumored to be having an affair with Tinkerbell, has been on base four times in the series, and has an eight-game hitting streak in the postseason. He also robbed Aurilia of a base hit Sunday and has played flawless defense.

E-Ticket Eckstein is so hopelessly immature that he runs out routine grounders, setting a dangerous tone for his ballclub.

As for the actual Rally Monkey, well, get used to it. The Angels' message board guys uncaged the Monkey in the bottom of the sixth, just before Garret Anderson singled home the tying run.

Has Willie Brown declared a boun... on Rally Monkeys?

Another factor to fear: K-Rod. Tha... would be Angels rookie relief pitche... Francisco Rodriguez, who spent the sea... son in the minors and has emerged i... the postseason as an absolute phenon...

The Angels brought the hard-throw... ing righty in Sunday at the start of th... sixth, and he retired all nine Giants h... faced, whiffing four. He got the win an... is now 5-0 in this postseason — Cin... derella in cleats.

For a two- or three-inning span, K... Rod is currently the world's most dev... astating and unhitable pitcher. Fear him...

Those are some elements over whic... the Giants will mull today on their da... off, along with:

■ How to get Barry Bonds mo... swings. Bonds walked three times Sun... day, once intentionally. He has yet t...

The lone Giants fan in his family, D.J. Larios, 8, opposite page, is surrounded by his Angel-loving sisters Mandy (left) and Imelda, all of West Covina, Calif., while waiting for tickets to Game 2. Opposite bottom, Rich Aurilia doubles in the fifth inning. Jeff Kent, below, launched one of six home runs hit in Game 2.

take a swing in this series with a runner on base.

The only time he has come to bat with a runner on — Sunday night when Aurilia was on second — naturally, the Angels walked Barry. The Angels occasionally pitch to Bonds, but they might be rethinking that misplaced machismo.

Why pitch to him Sunday in the ninth, with nobody on and a two-run lead? Don't they have cable in Anaheim?

■ How to eliminate the brain freezes. Reggie Sanders got caught leaning too far off second base on a ground ball to short. Benito Santiago made an ill-advised throw to second, allowing the runner on third to steal home. If these games are going to continue to be decided by one run, those goofs will be costly.

■ How to bring a strong home-field advantage to Pac Bell, to match the two-game grand mal tizzy thrown by the Anaheim fans. However, one hopes the Giants fans don't resort to the Sillystix that, while they sharpen the gross motor skills of the users, are man's most annoying invention.

■ Whether to admire or fear Dusty Baker's loyalty to his guys. It's easy to second-guess — which is why I'm doing it — but many impatient onlookers would not have allowed Giants starter Russ Ortiz to endure seven runs and nine hits before being permitted to shower. Baker finally yanked Ortiz with two out in the second, and Chad Zerbe quickly retired the first six Angels he faced.

Sometimes Baker's loyalty pays off. For example, Reggie Sanders, the nowhere man in the first two rounds of postseason, has two homers and four hits in the series.

The games resume Tuesday. Great stuff so far. May the farce be with us. ◆

Avenging Angels

OCT. 23, 2002

By Henry Schulman
CHRONICLE STAFF WRITER

Livan is leveled as Giants dumped in 2-1 hole

Perfection is for figure skaters and diamond cutters, not baseball players, who operate in a game that accepts failure as a natural part of the process.

Livan Hernandez's 6-0 career record in the postseason was impressive, but also a fat target for baseball's law of per-centages. Throw in Hernandez's knack for giving up runs in bunches, and it was clear that somebody was due to clean his clock.

The Anaheim Angels, who have a knack for scoring runs in bunches, were happy to make it happen in Game 3 of the World Series Tuesday night. They slapped Hernandez silly in a 10-4 victory at a misty Pacific Bell Park to grab a lead of two games to one in the Series.

"We've got to find a way over the next two games to keep their offense down," shortstop Rich Aurilia said. "Tonight we got our asses kicked.

"Are we down? No. Are we going to think about it tomorrow? No. We're going to go home, get a good night's sleep, have a good dinner and come back tomorrow. By no means is this Series over."

The Giants' challenge is daunting, though. They must win three of the final four games and at least once in Anaheim against a team with a 10,000-rpm offense.

It behooves them to take the final two games here lest they be forced to win two at Anaheim. The way the Angels have played there this postseason, the Giants might as well try to win two games down the street in Fantasyland.

In pummeling Russ Ortiz and Hernandez in successive games, the Angels have exploited one of the Giants' supposed advantages, their rotation.

Overall, Anaheim hitters scored 21 runs on 32 hits in winning Games 2 and 3, a rare double-whuppin' for the San Francisco staff.

"Their lineup is difficult because they have a lot of contact hitters," Hernandez said. "That team doesn't strike out too much, and for a pitcher who throws a lot of strikes, that's difficult."

Every Angels starter except pitcher

Ramon Ortiz had at least one hit, an Darin Erstad had three. First basema Scott Spiezio drove in three runs, two o a third-inning triple against Hernande

After scoring 11 runs to beat the G ants at home in Game 2, the Angel laughed in the face of predictions the could never tilt the scoreboard that wa in pitcher-friendly Pac Bell.

The Giants, who have seen the starters disappear in the second an fourth innings in the past two game need big innings from their starte tonight. The stopper's job falls to Kir Rueter, who is coming off six shutou innings against St. Louis in the clinch ing game of the NLCS, but he does no earn his money as an innings-eater.

"Obviously, when Kirk is on th mound, we feel good about ou chances," pitching coach Dave Righet said. "What you do is fight back, dig in

Outfielder Kenny Lofton is safe, above, on his steal past the tag of Angels second baseman Adam Kennedy in the first inning. Tony Bennett, left, finishes "America the Beautiful" as the Giants eyeball the Blue Angels. Top, Rose Woods of Vacaville watches the game from the trolley at Pacific Bell Park.

go after it and take someone down with you. We're going to go after them."

The Angels have set a postseason record by scoring 84 runs. On Tuesday night, they batted around in consecutive innings, a World Series first, scoring four runs in the third and four more in the fourth to take an 8-1 lead.

The Giants rallied in the fifth on homers by Aurilia and Barry Bonds, the latter with Jeff Kent aboard, cutting the lead to 8-4, but the Angels scored single runs off Aaron Fultz in the sixth and Scott Eyre in the eighth to banish any thoughts of a comeback.

Bonds set a record with his seventh home run of the postseason. He also became the first Giant ever to homer three times in a single World Series.

Babe Ruth's heirs might argue that the Bambino did not have the Division and League Championship Series with which to pad his stats. Now Bonds' heirs will be able to answer anyone who calls the man a postseason failure.

"I don't think anyone cares about those numbers right now," Aurilia said. "It's about winning. Barry could have hit four home runs tonight and it wouldn't have mattered."

The Giants' clubhouse was very quiet after this loss. Nobody raised a white flag, but after watching the Angels manhandle their pitching staff for the second straight game, the challenge ahead sank in quickly.

"They're a good offense. That's why they're here in the World Series," Kent said.

"We are too. We're just not keeping pace with them. It's a seven-game situation. We were kind of embarrassed tonight, but we'll strap it on tomorrow and see if we can't do better." ◆

GAME 3

Giants starter Livan Hernandez only lasted 3⅔ innings and Barry Bonds homered in his third consecutive World Series game

Giants style

S.F. shakes off two ugly losses to grind out a crucial Game 4 win

OCT. 24, 2002

By Henry Schulman
CHRONICLE STAFF WRITER

If only presidential elections were as black and white as this World Series. There is Angels baseball and Giants baseball, and there is no mistaking the two.

The Angels attack like fire ants, wave after wave, wearing down their prey with offense. The Giants keep things close and let their pitchers run the show until they get that perfectly timed hit.

San Francisco's style ruled in Game 4 at Pacific Bell Park on Wednesday night. As a result, this Series is tied 2-2.

David Bell, atoning for a bad running decision two innings earlier, singled home J.T. Snow with one out in the eighth inning against theretofore unbeatable rookie Francisco Rodriguez,

giving the Giants a 4-3 comeback win.

In winning a Series game in San Francisco for the first time since 1962, the Giants stopped what was beginning to look like a runaway Anaheim locomotive. They also reinforced a notion that might have gotten lost in the helter-skelter of Anaheim's wins in Games 2 and 3, that they have what it takes to beat the Angels.

"I think we needed to prove to ourselves more than anything that we could handle the pressure of the days before," Jeff Kent said after he helped the Giants close an early 3-0 deficit. "We needed our pitching staff to do what they did, what they've done in the past."

Kirk Rueter, making his World Series debut, allowed a run in the second on three successive hits and a David Eckstein sacrifice fly, and two more runs on a Troy Glaus homer in the third. Then he shut down Anaheim through the

sixth and completed the longest Series start by a Giant since Jack Sanford in Game 7, 1962.

Moreover, Rueter started the game-tying three-run rally in the fifth with a quirky infield hit. So often the Giants have turned to Rueter for an important game. So often he responds.

"What can I say about Kirk other than we love having him on the mound?" manager Dusty Baker said.

Thanks to Rueter, Bell, Snow, Kent, Kenny Lofton, Rich Aurilia and Benito Santiago, who all had a hand in the victory, the Series will return to Anaheim on Saturday. If the Giants can win tonight at Pac Bell behind Game 1 winner Jason Schmidt, they will go south needing one victory at Edison Field to take the Series.

Their cause will be helped immeasurably if Lofton and Aurilia can replicate what they did at the top of the order Wednesday night. After going a combined 4-for-26 in the first three games, they went 6-for-6 in the first five innings of Game 4.

Lofton also made a great running catch deep in center field to rob Tim Salmon of a leadoff double or triple in the eighth off Tim Worrell, who completed a 1-2-3 inning and earned the win.

Lofton and Aurilia started promising rallies in the first and third innings that died when the Angels walked Barry Bonds intentionally to load the bases with one out and Santiago hit into double plays. Santiago was so angry, he said, he smashed his helmet.

"When I hit into that second double play, I didn't want to go back to the dugout," Santiago said. "I wanted to jump up there and be with the fans. But you can't put your head down. I went back to the dugout and thought, 'Don't think about it. You might get a chance

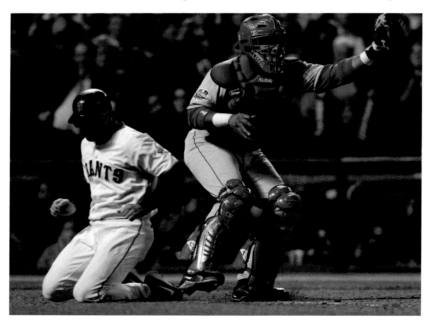

A pair of kayaking Santas, above, wait for a present from Barry Bonds in McCovey Cove outside Pacific Bell Park. Inside the park, J.T. Snow scores the winning run in the eighth inning, left. Jeff Passama (from left), Rubin Macias and Lucas Hansen bemoan the Angels decision to walk Bonds, top left, then celebrate the game-tying run.

o win the game.' "

Or at least tie it. Rueter started the fifth-inning rally off starter John Lackey with a two-strike chop off the plate that went 20 feet in front of the plate for an infield hit. That Rueter hit at all with the Giants down 3-0 raised some eyebrows.

Lofton then rolled a remarkable bunt up the third-base line. It hugged the line in air three-quarters of the way toward the bag. Glaus patiently waited for the ball to roll foul, and it did. As he bent down to grab it, though, the ball jerked back to the chalk — fair ball.

Aurilia then laced his third hit of the game to center to bring in Rueter. Kent's sacrifice fly to right got Lofton home, making it 3-2, and Aurilia took second when right fielder Salmon's throw was wide. Lackey walked Bonds intentionally again, a no-brainer after Santiago's two earlier double plays.

For Santiago, the third time was the charm. He lined a single to center to tie the game 3-3.

After perfect innings by Felix Rodriguez and Worrell in the seventh and eighth, it came down to the bottom of the eighth, against the Angels' Rodriguez, who had retired all 12 Giants he had faced in the Series.

Snow changed that, ripping a slider into right field for a single. Snow took second on a passed ball. Bell came to the plate one out later. With the game tied 3-3 in the sixth, Bell had singled down the left-field line to start the inning, but was thrown out handily by Garret Anderson trying to stretch it into a double.

"I wasn't happy about it because we needed a run right then," Bell said. "I was probably a little overaggressive. I never hit a ball like that that wasn't a double.

"That's no excuse. Anderson did a good job making the play. I can live with myself making an aggressive mistake, but it was still a mistake. I'm glad I got another opportunity."

Bell cashed it in, lining a single past

GAME 4
Kirk Rueter allowed 3 runs over 6 innings and the bullpen was perfect

GIANTS 4, ANGELS 3							
Anaheim	AB	R	H	BI	BB	SO	Avg.
Eckstein ss							
Erstad cf	3						
Salmon cf							
Giants	AB	R	H	BI	BB	SO	Avg.
Lofton cf	4	1	3	0	0	0	.250
Aurilia ss	4	1	3	1	0	0	.333
JKent 2b	3	0	0	1	0	2	.188
Bonds lf	1	0	0	0	3	0	.375
BSantiago c	4	0	1	1	0	0	.176
	4	1	1	0	0	0	.333

Giants	IP	H	R	ER	BB	SO	NP	ERA
Rueter	6	9	3	3	0	2	88	4.50
FRodriguez	1	0	0	0	0	1	9	3.60
Worrell W, 1-0	1	0	0	0	0	1	13	0.00
Nen S, 2	1	0	0	0	0	0	7	0.00
Worrell p								
REMartinez ph	1	0	0	0	0	1		
Nen p	0	0	0	0	0	0		

a diving shortstop David Eckstein that scored Snow with the go-ahead run.

Robb Nen made it stand up in the ninth, getting left-handed pinch-hitter Brad Fullmer to ground into a game-ending double play, making the first all-wild-card World Series all square. ◆

Final hit parade for the home fans

San Francisco can practice some steps, but don't start dancing yet

OCT. 25, 2002

You don't want to get too giddy yet. Trust us here. You want to take your psyche confidently into Game 6, but without too much of a swagger.

Remember, you were about ready to abandon the Giants yet again after Game 3. After Russ Ortiz and Livan Hernandez had been throttled to within an inch of their postseason careers, you feared the Anaheim Angels not only would win the World Series, but burn it to the ground.

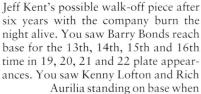

RAY RATTO

So you wait. And you wait. And you wait some more.

Oh, the hell with it. You just watched the boys mangle the Angels 16-4 in the most hyperactive display of World Se-

ries offense since 1960. You watched Jeff Kent's possible walk-off piece after six years with the company burn the night alive. You saw Barry Bonds reach base for the 13th, 14th, 15th and 16th time in 19, 20, 21 and 22 plate appearances. You saw Kenny Lofton and Rich Aurilia standing on base when Kent and Bonds did their damage. You saw J.T. Snow pull batboy Darren Baker out of harm's way while the Giants' conga line of baserunners rolled on into the night.

You will not listen to reason. You are partying like the Angels' team ERA is 19.99. You are so desperate to dance that you tried to find a 24-hour caterer.

You're not going to wait at all, and everybody in the house knows it.

So you stand on your roof and scream over the screams of your neighbors. The San Francisco Giants Are On The Verge Of Winning Their First World Series Ever! Forty-Eight Years Of Watching Champagne Happen To Someone Else Can End In 36 Hours! Willie McCovey Is Avenged! Loma Prieta Was Just The Earth Shifting In Its Seat A Little Bit! Order The Camembert And The Red Tail Ale, Margaret! It's Right There, So Close They Can Drink It!

But you still know it's wrong. The Angels have been cuffed around twice, and the face of their Series has turned from Tim Salmon and Scott Spiezio to Jarrod Washburn and Ben Weber, but they're still too hard-minded a team to take lightly. You assume the best at your peril.

Yes, you shriek, But They're Pitching Kevin Appier In Game Six. The Giants Don't Go Down To Kevin Appier. Ah, but this has not been a series for starting pitchers. It hasn't even been a

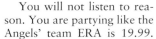

series for closers. Robb Nen has pitched twice in five games, Troy Percival once.

This World Series has been all about what the players call "raking." It is an amazement that players have not fought each other in the on-deck circle trying to get to the plate quickly enough.

This isn't elegant baseball, it's brute-force baseball. There isn't time to second-guess a manager, because you miss two more hits in the time it takes to instigate that "Let's put Shinjo in center and DH Lofton in Game 6" argument at the tavern.

This is, in fact, the first postseason in which the managers have been as helpless to affect the outcome as you or I or the accordion player. What, for example, was Mike Scioscia to do when Washburn topped his wretched start in Game 1 (18 balls in his first 26 pitches) with one incandescently worse (19 balls in his first 26 pitches, forced to intentionally walk Reggie Sanders, the man with the least discriminate strike zone on the Giants' roster)?

What, conversely, could Dusty Baker do to make his own lineup produce any more than it already has? The Giants

J.T. Snow drags manager Dusty Baker's son Darren, 3, away from homeplate, right, as he scores — closely followed by David Bell — in the seventh inning. Left, Rich Aurilia gets happy with Tsuyoshi Shinjo (right) after they both scored on Aurilia's homer to make the score 16-4. Above, Troy Glaus shows his frustration after striking out to end the first inning against Jason Schmidt.

are averaging 7.6 runs, 10.4 hits and nearly four extra-base hits per game. Benito Santiago is the only starter hitting below .280, and he's driving in a run a game.

This series is so Marlins-Indians 1997 that it almost looks like Yankees-Pirates 1960.

How can anyone with a black-and-orange rec room quibble with this? We refer you now to Kent, the designated bucket of cold water.

"This doesn't mean squat," he said, his exuberance fueled by his two homers and four RBIs. "This is one win we've gotten. We need to get one more."

And party-pooper extraordinaire though he might be (hey, he might be a Dodger next year, remember?), Kent is absolutely correct. Leading a series 3-2

did nothing for the Yankees last year, and they had momentum that wouldn't fit in the overhead bin. It did nothing for the Braves in '91, the Cardinals in '87, the Red Sox in '86, the Cardinals in '85 or the Brewers in '82.

On the other hand, it helped close the deal for the Marlins in '97, the Yankees in '96 and the Dodgers in '81.

Three-two means nothing. Well, that's a lie. Three-two makes for lousy beer. It also beats two-three. There isn't anyone who wouldn't rather pull for the Giants than the Angels given the present circumstances.

Still, we repeat, do not start dancing yet. You have miles to go before your heroes sleep. But it's OK to lean forward in your chair Saturday night. You know, just in case. ◆

GAME 5

Jeff Kent hit two home runs in their blow out victory

GIANTS 16, ANGELS 4

Anaheim	AB	R	H	BI	BB	SO	Avg.
Eckstein ss	4		2	1			
Erstad cf	4	0	1				
Salmon							

Giants	AB	R	H	BI	BB	SO	Avg.
Lofton cf	6	3	3	2	0	0	.318
Eyre p	0	0	0	0	0	1	.333
Aurilia ss	6	2	2	3	0	1	.286
JKent 2b	5	4	3	4	1	0	.500
Bonds lf	3	2	0	1	3	1	.200
BSantiago c	3	1	0	0	1	1	.313
RSanders rf	1	0	0	0	0	0	---
FRodriguez p	1	0	0	0	0	1	.167
Dunston ph	1	0	0	0	0	0	
Worrell p	0	0	0	0	0	0	
Feliz ph	1	0	0	0	0	0	
Goodwin rf	4	2	2	2	0	0	
Snow 1b	4	2	3				

Out-rallied

Angels' monkey perched on Giants' backs as they give up late 5-0 lead

OCT. 27, 2002

By Henry Schulman
CHRONICLE STAFF WRITER

ANAHEIM — It has been a hallmark of Dusty Baker's teams the last six seasons. The bigger they fall, the better they get. Break their heart one night, they'll break yours the next. Or so it says on the brochures.

If the Giants are to win the 2002 World Series, they will have to live up to that billing in ways they never could have imagined.

On a clear, chilly evening at Edison Field, the Giants were eight outs from their first Series championship since the team moved to San Francisco. They had a 5-0 lead. They silenced the rabid Anaheim crowd. They could taste it.

Instead, they tasted their most bitter defeat. A seemingly harmless single by Troy Glaus with one out in the seventh inning started a ferocious Anaheim comeback. The Angels stormed back to win 6-5, going ahead on Glaus' two-run double off Robb Nen with nobody out in the eighth inning.

Anaheim's Game 6 victory tied the Series at three wins apiece, setting up a decisive Game 7 tonight. It will be hard enough for the Giants to digest Saturday night's failure without considering the historic wall that stands in their way.

The last seven teams that tried to win Game 7 of a World Series on the road have failed.

"We've been doing this since mid-August," losing pitcher Tim Worrell said. "It comes down to one game. It kind of stinks after the way tonight's game went that it comes down to one game. On the other hand, we can still come back and win this thing."

When the Giants took a 5-0 lead in the top of the seventh on Jeff Kent's two-out RBI single, their dugout went wild. Anyone who said they did not start thinking ahead to the party at that moment must have been fibbing.

Then again, these Angels have been so explosive, a comeback had to be in the back of their minds.

Shawon Dunston, at 39 the Giants' oldest player and most tenured major-leaguer, got them rolling with a two-run homer off Kevin Appier in the fifth inning, breaking a scoreless tie.

Barry Bonds, never shy about discussing his thirst for a ring, later hit his fourth homer of the Series, deep into the right-field seats, against Francisco Rodriguez. Kenny Lofton, the last piece of the puzzle who arrived in July, used his bat and legs to provide two more runs. When Kent singled Lofton home with two out in the seventh, the Giants had their 5-0 lead.

The way Russ Ortiz was pitching, that lead seemed as safe as the gold in Fort Knox.

Ortiz overcame the miseries of his first Series start and pitched shutout baseball on two hits through six innings.

When Ortiz allowed back-to-back singles by Troy Glaus and Brad Fullmer with one out in the seventh, Baker called on Felix Rodriguez in a crucial and controversial move given how well Ortiz was throwing.

Rodriguez has been the Giants' unsung hero this postseason, pitching in all six Series games and 13 of 16 postseason games. Scott Spiezio worked Rodriguez for nine pitches, finally hitting a high fly down the right-field line for a three-run homer that mirrored Dunston's two-run homer to left earlier.

Suddenly, it was a 5-3 game, and 44,506 fans had hope.

Worrell got the last out of the seventh, but when Darin Erstad took him deep to start the eighth, the lead was down to 5-4. Tim Salmon and Garret Anderson followed with bloop singles to center and left, respectively, and when Bonds bobbled and kicked Anderson's ball for an error, Anderson moved to second.

Baker, needing a strikeout right then and six more outs overall, called for Nen. But Glaus slammed a pitch into the gap in left-center, scoring Salmon and Anderson with the tying and go-ahead runs.

Nen got three outs to give his team a fighting chance against Troy Percival in the ninth, but to no avail. The Angels' closer finished the job 1-2-3, the Series was tied 3-all and the Giants were left to scratch their heads, figure out what happened and quickly forget it.

"We had three or four of our best pitchers out there, and they scored six runs in the last two or three innings," Kent said. "With this team you've still got to go get 'em, stick it to 'em and make sure they're down and out, not just down." ◆

Benito Santiago sits in the dugout in the ninth inning, opposite page. Above, Shawon Dunston Jr. greets Shawon Dunston Sr. after the father's fifth-inning home run.

GAME 6
Shawon Dunston started the scoring with a two-run home run

...ering a 3-run home run
seventh inning, cutting the Gia...

ANGELS 6, GIANTS 5

Giants	AB	R	H	BI	BB	SO	Avg.
Lofton cf	5	2	2	0	0	0	.333
Aurilia ss	4	0	2	1	1	2	.286
JKent 2b	4	0	1	1	0	1	.320
Bonds lf	2	1	1	1	2	1	.500
BSantiago c	3	0	0	0	1	0	.174
Snow 1b	4	0	1	0	0	3	.348
RSanders rf	4	0	0	0	0	0	.250
DaBell 3b	4	1	1	0	0	0	.350
Dunston dh	3	1	1	2	0	1	.222
Goodwin ph	1	0	0	0	0	0	.000
Totals	**34**	**5**	**8**	**4**	**4**	**10**	

Heartbreaker

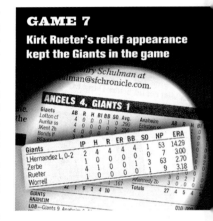
Series drought continues for Giants when team fails to bounce back from Game 6

OCT. 28, 2002

By Henry Schulman
CHRONICLE STAFF WRITER

ANAHEIM — There is an insurmountable problem with the whole "team of destiny" thing. Every club that reaches the World Series feels it owns the copyright, but one of the two always is going to lose.

After so many weeks of joy and success, the end is painful beyond words.

So it was for the 2002 Giants, who were so close to the championship they could shut their eyes and imagine the diamonds that would have adorned those golden rings. Instead, a season of great accomplishment ended like many before it, another notch in the franchise's long time line of disappointment.

The fifth-longest World Series championship drought in the majors reached 48 years Sunday night when the Anaheim Angels defeated the Giants 4-1 and won the title, four games to three.

In capturing their first Series since their inception in 1961, the Angels joined the 1997 Florida Marlins as the only wild cards to win one.

Now, the Giants have months to absorb the pain of losing a championship they were eight outs from winning before the Angels stunned them with a six-run comeback in Game 6.

For players such as Barry Bonds, Shawon Dunston, Kenny Lofton and Benito Santiago, this might have been their last chance to snag baseball's ultimate prize.

"I'm heartsick that some of these folks may not have a chance to do this again," general manager Brian Sabean said. "They played as hard as they could … but they came up against a team that had a lot going for them."

The Series defeat might have implications far beyond 2002. It could spell the end of manager Dusty Baker's tenure in San Francisco after 10 seasons. His decision to return and the club's decision to rehire him hinge on so many factors.

In the Angels, the Giants ran into the kind of offensive buzz saw they never encountered during the regular season or the NL playoffs. It was too much for Livan Hernandez. Baker gave the Game 7 start to Hernandez over Kirk Rueter on three days' rest, a decision that will be debated for ages after what occurred. The Angels pounded Hernandez for four runs in two-plus innings. Garret Anderson's three-run double to right busted open a 1-1 game in the third, the last hit Hernandez would allow in 2002.

Later, Rueter pitched four innings of one-hit, shutout relief.

Meanwhile, the Giants' offense was stumped by Angels rookie John Lackey and relievers Brendan Donnelly, Francisco Rodriguez and Troy Percival. They scored their only run on a second-inning sacrifice fly by Sanders.

They did fight to the last, putting two runners on base in the ninth against Percival. The game, Series and season ended with Lofton's drive to right-center.

"We went up against a team — and this is going to sound like a stupid word — of destiny," Jeff Kent said. "It seemed like everything just went their way and we couldn't cue it up."

Ultimately, the Giants know this Series will not be remembered for Anderson's three-run double. Instead, it will be remembered for the 5-0, seventh-inning lead they blew in Game 6.

As Aurilia said, "We lost Game 6. They beat us in Game 7."

One man whose eyes were dry was Dunston, who had bawled like a baby the night the Giants won the National League pennant.

"I cried then because I never made it to a World Series. I was like, 'Wow!' " Dunston said. "I don't mean any disrespect, but I can't cry right now because I'm still going to get a ring, a National League championship ring, and I'm going to wear that proudly. Trust me." ◆

Giants hitter Tom Goodwin sits silently in the dugout, right, as Angels fans rejoice after the game. A pensive Barry Bonds awaits a pitching change in the third inning, top; far left, the Angels celebrate after the last out.

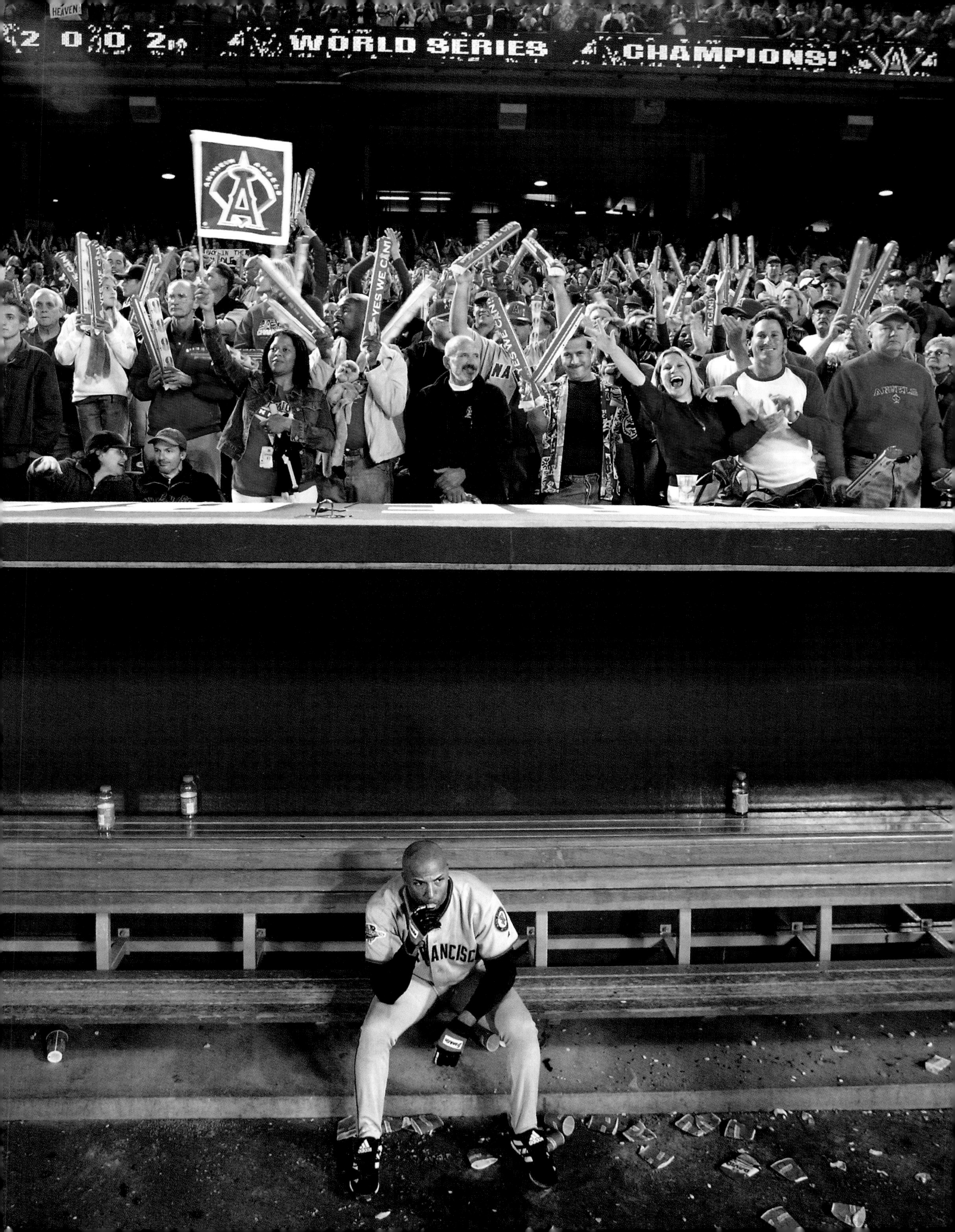
2002 WORLD SERIES CHAMPIONS!
HEAVEN
YES WE CAN
ANGELS

Cheers, tears for the season past

5,000 fans rally for Giants team that came so close

*By Brian Murphy
and Carl Nolte*
CHRONICLE STAFF WRITERS

The sun shone all over Pacific Bell Park on Monday, spreading a warm, sympathetic glow on the Giants and some 5,000 die-hard fans assembled for a post-World Series rally. Surveying the pristine sky and breathing the fresh, late-October air, the Giants and all assembled had to have the same nagging, heavy thought:

It would have been a great day for a parade.

Dusty Baker, surely, was thinking along those lines. The emotion of the scene, and his very uncertain future with the Giants, overtook the 10-year skipper at the close of the rally, and he broke down, crying as he carried his 3-year-old son, Darren, toward the team bus waiting down the left-field line.

Baker never spoke at the rally, only waving to a crowd that lovingly chanted his name over, and over. Reporters tried to get Baker to talk, but he could barely choke out words, saying only, "I'm sad" and, when asked about Darren, saying "He'll be OK."

Broadcaster Jon Miller, who emceed the mostly upbeat 30-minute farewell to the National League champions, was asked why Baker did not speak.

"I asked him if he wanted to," Miller said, "but he said he'd get too emotional. He said he would break down."

A few feet away from Miller, Baker moved slowly to the bus, and from underneath his sunglasses, tears trickled down his cheeks. Monday, apparently, was too soon to process the pain of a seven-game Series loss to the Anaheim Angels. When the Giants arrived at the field for the rally, it had been just 16 hours since Darin Erstad caught Kenny Lofton's fly ball to end Game 7.

Shortstop Rich Aurilia said Baker went around the clubhouse on Sunday night after Game 7, congratulating each player on a fine season, and added that he understood why the skipper passed on speaking on Monday. Aurilia, too, briefly choked up in his speech at the rally.

"It's hard to come out here and talk in front of all these people who look at you as a leader," Aurilia said. "Especially in Dusty's case, when you don't know what the future holds."

Asked if anyone had lobbied for Baker to stay, Aurilia said: "I think about 10,000 (actually 5,000) people just did."

Owner Peter Magowan, whose reported friction with Baker is believed to be the reason Baker does not have a new deal, paid tribute to the manager in his speech to the crowd, saying: "There are a lot of people I want to thank, starting with our great manager, Dusty Baker."

Nobody spoke for the fans. Nobody had to. Just being in the ballpark, one could feel the affection roll out of the stands like the fog on those cold nights at Candlestick years ago.

"I'm sad, I'm in mourning, but I'm here to celebrate a great season," said Celina Gomes, 20, of San Francisco.

"I love the team because they play with all their heart. They play baseball the way you are supposed to live your life," she said. "With passion, with fun."

Inside the office of longtime equipment manager Mike Murphy sat Giants legend Willie McCovey, himself a veteran of World Series pain. Murphy walked in and saw Stretch, remembering the line drive into Bobby Richardson's glove to end the 1962 World Series.

"I was hoping we'd win for you," Murphy said to McCovey. "Remember '62?"

"I wish we could have written a different script this year," McCovey said, "but it didn't happen."

McCovey shook his head. His heartbreak came in the final game, but Stretch had a feeling that as the winter rains come, the Giants will think more and more about that 5-0 lead in the seventh inning of Game 6.

"I think Game 6 is going to hurt for a long time," McCovey said. "For that club (in '62), it's Game 7. For this club, it's Game 6.

"They'll think about it, and have recurring dreams about it." ◆

W. BEHRENDS 2000

Giants fan Matt Manfre, 10, of Watsonville waits in line for the rally near the Willie Mays statue outside Pacific Bell Park, above. Some players cleaned out their lockers Monday, left, including Tsuyoshi Shinjo (right). Opposite page, Dusty Baker gives his son, Darren, a kiss during the rally.

Batboy Darren Baker, 3, and his father, Giants manager Dusty Baker, trot out of the clubhouse at the start of Game 4 of the World Series at Pacific Bell Park. Darren became a good-luck charm for the team during the regular season.